THE PURSUITS
OF PHILOSOPHY

THE PURSUITS OF PHILOSOPHY

An Introduction to the Life and Thought
of David Hume

Annette C. Baier

HARVARD UNIVERSITY PRESS
Cambridge, Massachusetts, and London, England
2011

3/12
25.00

Printed in the United States of America

Library of Congress Cataloging-in-Publication Data

Baier, Annette.
The pursuits of philosophy : an introduction to the life and thought
of David Hume / Annette C. Baier.
p.   cm.
Includes bibliographical references (p.   ) and indexes.
ISBN 978-0-674-06168-2 (alk. paper)
1. Hume, David, 1711–1776.   I. Title.
B1498.B25   2011
192—dc22   2011012315

CONTENTS

Introduction   1

1   Childhood and Youth:
    Loss of Faith and a Passion
    for Literature   6

2   "At a Distance from Relations":
    Writing His *Treatise* in France   15

3   Hume after the *Treatise*   55

4   Hume as Librarian and Historian   84

5   Hume's Life as a Man in the
    Public Eye   102

6   Hume's Final Years in Edinburgh   116

7 Death and Character   124

   Afterword   134

   Annotated Bibliography   147

   Further Reading   151

   Acknowledgments   155

   Name Index   157

   Subject Index   161

NOTE ON REFERENCES

Hume's works in the text will observe the following abbreviations:

E   *Enquiries Concerning Human Understanding and Concerning the Principles of Morals,* 3rd ed., edited by L. A. Selby-Bigge, revised text and notes by P. H. Nidditch (Oxford: Clarendon Press, 1975), giving page number.

Ess *Essays Moral, Political, and Literary,* edited by Eugene Miller (Indianapolis: Liberty Press, 1985), giving page number.

H   *A History of England,* 6 vols. (Indianapolis: Liberty Press, 1983), giving volume number and page number.

L   *Letters of David Hume,* 2 vols., edited by J. Y. T. Greig (Oxford: Clarendon Press, 1939–1969), giving volume number and page number.

NL *New Letters of David Hume,* edited by Raymond
Klibansky and Ernest C. Mossner (Oxford:
Clarendon Press, 1954), giving page number.

T   *A Treatise of Human Nature,* 2nd ed., edited by
L. A. Selby-Bigge, revised text and variant
readings by P. H. Nidditch (Oxford: Clarendon
Press, 1978), giving page number.

THE PURSUITS
OF PHILOSOPHY

INTRODUCTION

David Hume's life is an oft-told tale. He wrote
it up for us, in very brief compass, in the last year
of his life, and I shall incorporate what he wrote
here, quoting from it at the start of each of my chapters, and omitting none of it. Smellie, Ritchie, Burton, Huxley, Stephen, and Knight in the nineteenth
century; Orr, Greig, Mossner, and Streminger in
the twentieth century; and Graham in this century
have all found Hume's life worth their efforts. And
others, such as Hill in his 1888 edition of Hume's
letters to his publisher, Strahan, and Ayer, Price,
and Capaldi, in their twentieth-century books about
Hume's thought, have included brief biographies,
Capaldi's giving an illuminating time line, locating
Hume's life in relation to writings that influenced
him, such as Berkeley's *Principles* the year before
Hume's birth, and to what was written in reaction to
him, such as Price's *A Review of the Principal Questions
of Morals*. In 2010, Kenneth Merrill gave us an A–Z of

Hume, with some attention to his life and the social conditions in which he lived. Hume must be the most biographer-inspiring philosopher to have lived. So what is left to say?

My main aim is to try to connect the life with the thought, something that has been done (a little) by Mossner and Streminger in the most complete biographies we have, less by Greig, whose lively and sympathetic account of Hume's life and thought is soundly based on his letters, which he had edited, but which does not include a summary of his views. Merrill's book restricts itself to the content of Hume's first philosophical works and does not cover his essays and histories. The combined task of dealing with both life and thought will be done more thoroughly by James Harris in his forthcoming intellectual biography of Hume, commissioned by Oxford University Press. His will be a book for experts, while my little book is for the general reader who has some interest in what philosophy is and in how one great philosopher lived his life. For information about that life I rely mainly on Hume's own autobiography, his letters, and what his other biographers have written. I make no pretensions to new biographical discoveries, and what I say is best construed as simply commentary on what Hume himself told us. What this book adds to Greig's fine book is mainly a summary of Hume's views and commentary on them. And I am aware that this commentary often expresses purely personal tastes, just as my summary of his views expresses only *my* considered opinion as to what was meant. I am aware that other Hume readers have differing interpretations and would have made different comments.

Hume was a great philosopher, even if he liked, later in life, to be known as a historian. And he wrote very well, as is not true of most philosophers. His *History of England* is imbued with the concerns of his moral and political philosophy and so is a kind of applied philosophy. After his nervous breakdown in youth, Hume wrote in his famous letter to a physician that the moral philosophy of the ancients, with their "beautiful Representations of Virtue and Philosophy" (L 1:14), was not based on an understanding of our nature, and any useful ethics had to be so based, so his study of our nature was all along a preparation for his "moral conclusions." Not that his views in ethics were static, and even within the *History* itself there are changes in attitude to such matters as religious superstition and ritual, dealt with quite kindly when Hume considers Archbishop William Laud and his trial and execution (H 5:458–

460) and not so kindly in the later volumes he wrote on the medieval period. In his Tudor volumes he had been condemnatory of Henry VIII for trying the bones of Thomas à Becket for treason (H 3:254), but when he comes to deal with Becket himself, he is so scathing that, once these volumes were translated into Italian, all his works were quickly put on the index of prohibited books (H 1:336). His attitude to religion, throughout his life and writings, is one of the things that I shall try to chart. Another that I shall attend to is his version of our nature as human beings, the topic of his first work. There the treatment was abstruse and general, and in some ways it is a pity he did not redo it, after his close study of the rulers of England and his own dealings with many people, of several nationalities, in the course of his life. He ended a pessimist, at least about the prospects for the English, while when he was younger he had hoped he could influence British culture for the better, the less factious, and the less bigoted.

Hume ended his life cheering on the American rebels, or at least thinking it futile for Britain to try to defeat them, and his hopes for an understanding of his philosophy and his ideals were placed in people like Benjamin Franklin, who had been his guest in Edinburgh. He wrote to Franklin in 1772, "I expected, in entering on my literary course, that all the Christians, all the Whigs, and all the Tories, would be my enemies. But it is hard that all the English, Irish and Welsh should also be against me. The Scotch likewise cannot be much my friends, as no man is a prophet in his own country. However it is some consolation that I can bear up my head under all this prejudice. I fancy that I must have recourse to America for justice" (L 2:258; NL 194). The size of the membership of the Hume Society in the North American continent, where it began, and the regular issuing there of *Hume Studies,* would surely have pleased the man whose work is studied. Hume's *Treatise* has been translated into many languages, most recently into Latvian, and Jonathan Bennett has even translated it into contemporary English. Many of us, in many lands and languages, have tried, in our commentaries, to do Hume justice, for he has wisdom to offer. This book tries to communicate a little of Hume's wisdom to a wider audience than those few who share the young Hume's taste for "abstruse" thinking, since his hope was that a sound philosophy could "diffuse itself through the whole society."

1

CHILDHOOD AND YOUTH

Loss of Faith and a Passion for Literature

It is difficult for a man to speak long about himself without vanity; therefore I shall be short. It may be thought an instance of vanity that I pretend at all to write my life; but this Narrative shall contain little more than the History of my Writings; as indeed almost all my life has been spent in literary pursuits and occupations. The first success of most of my writings was not such as to be an object of vanity.

I was born the 26th of April, 1711, old style, at Edinburgh. I was of good family, both by father and mother: my father's family is a branch of the Earl of Home's, or Hume's; and my ancestors have been proprietors of the estate, which my brother possesses, for several generations. My mother was daughter of Sir David Falconer, President of the college of Justice: the title of Lord Halkerton came by succession to her brother.

My family, however, was not rich, and being myself a younger brother, my patrimony, according to the mode of my country, was of course very slender. My father, who passed for a man of parts, died when I was an infant, leaving me, with an elder brother and sister, under the care of our mother, who, though young and handsome, devoted herself entirely to the rearing and educating of her children. I passed through the ordinary course of education with success, and was seized very early with a passion for literature, which has been the ruling passion of my life, and the great source of my enjoyments. My studious disposition, and my industry, gave my family a notion that the law was a proper profession for me; but I found an unsurmountable aversion to everything but the pursuits of philosophy and general learning: and while they fancied I was poring over Voet and Vinnius, Cicero and Virgil were the authors which I was secretly devouring.

David Hume was, as he tells us, born in Edinburgh in 1711 on April 26, "old style" (on May 7, by our Gregorian calendar, only adopted in Britain in 1752), the third child and second son of Joseph Home (pronounced "Hume") and Katherine Falconer, daughter of Sir David Falconer, who had been chief justice in Scotland. Hume writes in his *Treatise* that the strongest tie the human mind is capable of is the love of parents for their children, and his mother showed that love, but his father died in his infancy. His parents had grown up together on the family estate, Ninewells, by the Whitadder or Whitewater River at Chirnside, near Berwick, as Katherine's mother had been third wife to Joseph Home's father. They shared no ancestor, so their relationship was not a case of incest. But the fact that they had grown up in one home, as brother and sister, helps us understand the near obsession that David Hume displayed, in his writings, with incest prohibitions and the reasons for them. If, as he suggested, one good reason for such prohibitions is that family relations are corrupted if sexual love is treated as a possibility between any family members except the married couples in the household, then he must have wondered about the innocence of the adolescence of his own parents. Philosophy begins in wonder at what is familiar and closest, and the young Hume, who loved and greatly admired his mother but had no memory of his father, must have wondered both at the fact that she, once she was a widow, "though young and handsome, devoted herself entirely to the rearing and education of her children," and at the fact that her one adult love and husband had been her stepbrother, with whom she had grown up. He gives little attention to wonder as a human phenomenon, but that does not mean he never felt it.

Scotland in Hume's time was a God-fearing nation. Hume told James Boswell how he puzzled over the list of sins that he was encouraged as a child to examine himself for, in particular, the sin of pride. This list is to be found in *The Whole Duty of Man,* a tract produced a half century before by an Anglican divine, Joseph Allestree. Hume's mother's family was Anglican, so he had both Presbyterian and Anglican influences on him in youth. He told Boswell he skipped quickly over the sections in the *Whole Duty* on murder and theft, having no inclination to engage in them. But pride was another matter. He excelled at his studies, and entered university at the same time as his elder brother, but was taught that it was sinful to take the pleasure of pride in his intellectual achievements. He was the younger son, so the estate passed to his elder brother, and his own patrimony was "slender." In his later political philosophy and history, he spells out the reasons why the practice of letting the eldest son inherit all the property of his father makes good social sense, but as a young man he must have wondered why he, the cleverest of the three children, should not inherit more of what their father left. That he would likely have been bored administering a rural estate was one thing; that he remained, into his thirties, "a poor philosopher," dependent on his mother and elder brother for a home, was another and a more galling one. His later account of "justice" emphasizes the element of arbitrariness in many social rules, and he had good personal reason to have pondered the rules on inheritance.

"I passed through the ordinary course of education with success," Hume tells us. Such a course, at Edinburgh University, where he went at age 10 or 11, taught him Latin and a little Greek, logic, ethics, divinity, and some "natural philosophy," through which he was introduced to the theories of Isaac Newton. Hume went on to study law but "found an unsurmountable aversion to everything except the pursuits of philosophy and general learning." His indulgent family let him give up law and devote himself to trying to express in writing the "whole new scene of thought," which he said, in a long and probably unsent "letter to a physician" about his ill health in youth (L 1:16), broke in upon him at about age 18. He gave himself up to "the pursuits of philosophy" and scribbled away quires of paper, leaving the running of his home estate to his mother, brother, and sister. We can only speculate about what this new scene of thought was. It may have been connected to his conclusion that the "beautiful representations of virtue" in the ancient moralists (Cicero and Virgil) he told the physician he had been reading were not based on an understanding of human nature, yet only if they were so based could such representations inspire human conduct to conform to them. Before any ethics can be formulated for the likes of us, we must first understand our own nature and do so after careful empirical study, not just by accepting dogmas about original sin or definitions of us as rational animals. So Hume's first book was *A Treatise of Human Nature*. As he told the physician to whom he wrote this long letter in 1734, he suffered a breakdown of health while at home, and he did not actually get his book written till he left Ninewells and, after a brief and unsuccessful try at "a more active scene of life" with a sugar importer in Bristol, went to France to settle to write. He needed not only some physical activity (at home he had taken to riding eight or ten miles a day) but also a new scene, not the home scene, to do justice to his "new scene of thought."

Part of the reason for the psychosomatic ill health that had dogged him in his last years at home may have been connected not just with his failed attempts to live up to fine pagan ideals of good character but also with his loss of religious faith. He had been given a Christian upbringing, and the Bible would have been one of the first books he was encouraged to read.

His uncle was minister at the local Chirnside church, where sinners were put in the pillory. Heresy trials were conducted in the area; during Hume's youth, one such trial would have been that of William Dudgeon. Later in life, when he was working on his *Dialogues on Natural Religion,* Hume wrote to his friend Gilbert Elliot that he had just burned an old manuscript written before he was 20, containing his thoughts about theism. "It began with an anxious search after arguments, to confirm the common opinion: doubts stole in, dissipated, returned, were again dissipated, returned again." He said that his inclination, at that time, was to believe in God but that reading the defenses of Christianity by Locke and Clarke undermined rather than strengthened his faith. Seeing the bigotry of the local clergy must also have played a role. Shortly after he left home, a young servant woman, Agnes Galbraith, pregnant out of wedlock, was put in the Chirnside pillory. She named David Hume as the father of her child but for some reason does not seem to have been believed. That such things went on would be one reason why David Hume became convinced not only that there was no reason to believe the religious dogmas he had been taught but that religion, and in particular the Christian religion, was a force against, not for, a humane morality. Since his mother and sister were pious, this conviction must have made for some difficulty at home. Still, he always returned there gladly after any time away. Theologian biographer James Orr, who, after writing his book on Hume, went on to write books on the defacement of the image of God in modern man and on sin, shows understanding of the sincerity of the young Hume's gropings with the question of how to live and what role religion should play in life, just as he, unlike some others, also understands what Hume's mother meant when she described her famous son as "a fine good-natured creature, but uncommon wake-minded." Orr was a Scot, and he assumes (as later writers including David Norton, most recent editor of Hume's philosophical works, did not) that "wake [weak]-minded" meant "weak-willed" (in his *Treatise,* Hume himself uses its opposite, "strength of mind," to mean strength of will) and that this was a reasonable judgment for a worried mother to make of the young son who persevered neither with his law studies nor with his trial of business. He kept indulging his love of writing, despite the need to find some profitable occupation. Was it to escape her judgment that Hume left home? He wrote in his *Treatise* that those who are ashamed of their poverty or lack of success often choose to live among strangers, since "we are most uneasy under the contempt of persons who are both related by blood and contiguous in place. Hence we seek to diminish this sympathy and uneasiness by separating these relations, and placing ourselves in a contiguity with strangers and at a distance from relations" (T 322). It is our relatives' sympathy with our distress and our own sympathy with their disappointment which is partly what hurts. Sympathy, in Hume's view of it, is a most important feature of our nature, a near-automatic sharing of the sentiments of those whose faces and body language we can see and read. The sympathy of a mother for her unhappy son, the would-be writer, would be as hard to bear as was his own sympathy for her concern about what his place in life was to be. Orr shows this understanding of the young Hume's predicament when living at home as a not-yet-published writer, as do some other biographers such as Greig, who even thinks Hume's family had become hostile to him and that his elder brother virtually evicted him. I doubt Hume would have shown as much affection to them later as he did had that been the case. Nor would he have written so eloquently in his *Treatise* about the strength of family love.

2

"AT A DISTANCE FROM RELATIONS"

Writing His Treatise *in France*

My very slender fortune, however, being unsuitable to this plan of life, and my health being a little broken by my ardent application, I was tempted, or rather forced, to make a very feeble trial of entering into a more active scene of life. In 1734 I went to Bristol, with some recommendation to eminent merchants, but in a few months found that scene totally unsuitable to me. I went over to France, with a view of prosecuting my studies in a country retreat; and I there laid that plan of life, which I have steadily and successfully pursued. I resolved to make a very rigid frugality supply my deficiency of fortune, to maintain unimpaired my independency, and to regard every object as contemptible, except the improvement of my talents in literature.

During my retreat in France, first in Reims, but chiefly at La Fleche, in Anjou, I composed my Treatise of Human Nature. *After passing three years, very agreeably in that*

country, I came over to London in 1737. In the end of 1738 I
published my Treatise *and immediately went down to my*
mother and my brother, who lived in his country house,
and was employing himself very judiciously and success-
fully in the improvement of his fortune.

Never literary attempt was more unfortunate than my
Treatise of Human Nature. *It fell* dead-born from
the press, *without reaching the distinction, as even to ex-*
cite a murmur among the zealots. But being naturally of a
cheerful and sanguine temper, I very soon recovered from
the blow, and prosecuted with great ardour my studies in
the country.

When Hume went to France in September 1734, he
lived at first in Paris, then for a while in Rheims,
where he had some letters of introduction and wrote
back to his friend, Michael Ramsay, comparing
French and English customs of polite address. Such
customs he later called "small morals," likening
them to the rules of justice. The latter stop collisions
of different persons' interests, while good manners
protect everyone's pride. He finally settled in as a
lodger in a small chateau, Yvandeau, near La Flèche,
where there was an excellent library in the Jesuit College, where Descartes had been educated. (Did this
fact influence Hume to live there? He did tell Michael

Yvandeau, La Flèche, where Hume wrote his *Treatise*. Photographed by the author.

Ramsay to read Descartes, to appreciate what Hume himself was saying in his *Treatise*.) There he tried out his argument on the credibility of reports of miracles on the monks, whom he reports were "gravelled" by it. The argument, as he later gives it, is that miracles have to be contrary to what we take to be natural laws, but these must have the best possible evidence to count as such laws. However good the character of someone who claims to have witnessed a miracle, the chances that he is mistaken or deluded are always higher than the possibility that the laws of nature have been broken. Our rule should be always to accept the lesser miracle—only if it would be more of a miracle for this testifier to be wrong than that the hitherto unbroken law should have been broken should we accept the miracle report. But as he told Henry Home (later Lord Kames), Hume decided not to include this argument in his *Treatise,* foreseeing that it might show him as the infidel he was (NL 2). He also intended to show the work to Bishop Butler, and did not wish to offend his religious sensibilities. It is a strange thought: the large, clumsy, studious young Scot, with his poor French, trying to persuade the French Jesuits that there was always more reason to disbelieve than to believe a miracle report. Indeed, his whole time in France, as an impoverished would-be author living among strangers, must have strained his fortitude and tested his resolve. But he wrote on and by September 1737 could return to London to find a publisher. It took him a year to do so, and that must have been a very nerve-wracking year.

So what was his account of human nature? Aristotle had defined us as the rational animal, but Christian accounts of our nature had stressed not our reason but our sinful passions, which were to be disciplined by God-given conscience and by respect for religious tradition, which taught that we have immortal souls, whose salvation should be our main concern. Hume's wholly secular account keeps the stress on our passions, and he sees reason as their servant. Our main concern, he thinks, should be to live well during this life, which is all we have and in which the quality of one person's life is always entangled with that of those around him or her, so our concern has to be for *our* lives. Our capacity for sympathy alone ensures some degree of this entanglement, and our moral sense increases it. Hume's *Treatise* includes three books, one on our understanding, one on our passions, one on morals. Two more were first projected, on politics and on taste. But the indifferent reception to the first three deterred him from writing the last two, and it is to his later essays and dissertations that we must turn to find his views about those topics. One of his most infamous theses was his endorsement of Hobbes's claim that our reason serves our passions, so to define us as the rational animal, or, as Descartes had, as a thinking thing, is to misperceive the relative roles of thought and of passion. All intelligent animals, Hume claimed, use their reason to help them pursue their ends, and we are different mainly in that language makes a difference to the form our reason can take, making us capable of conversation, science, philosophy and history. Like all other surviving animals, we learn from experience and remember the lessons of past experience. Unlike other animals, we can share our experience by speech and writing, though Hume, like Descartes, is rather scathing about the beliefs we acquire from education in the form of indoctrination, and he tends to stress our own experience as the best teacher. He tells us (T 8) that the reason why he must begin with our ideas and our understanding is that ideas are involved in our passions, which are what chiefly concern him. Hobbes thought our strongest passion was fear of death, but Hume tries to persuade us that, unless it is violent, painful, or very premature, death should hold no terror for us, as it would if a final judgment and a hell awaited us. (This teaching is found not in the *Treatise*, which puts no stress on fear of death, but in his essays such as that on suicide and on the immortality of the soul [Ess 577–598]).

Hume advised his friend Michael Ramsay to read Descartes, as well as Malebranche and Bayle, as preparation for reading what Hume himself had written. Descartes, too, wrote about our passions, but it was not that work, *The Passions of the Soul*, that Hume advised Ramsay to read, but rather the *Meditations*, to which Hume's *Treatise* is a sort of inverse mirror, beginning where Descartes ended, with some trust in our senses and passions as, if he is right, the origins of all our ideas; Hume then works his way to a subsequent skepticism of the senses, whereas Descartes had begun with a resolve to distrust the senses until he found firmer foundations for his beliefs. By the end of Book I, Hume finds himself in an "express contradiction," outlawing the very reasoning which had led him to this desperate move, while Descartes' initial and provisional skepticism had been banished the moment he realized that it would be an express contradiction to claim "I am not now thinking, nor claiming anything." Hume enacts a beautiful inversion of Descartes' procedure. He ends Book I a skeptic, one who has found no coherent account of what he himself is. But he nevertheless goes on to look at human passions, which he had begun by saying were his chief concern, and on examination finds them less likely to induce skepticism.

In Book I, before the skepticism set in, Hume gave a famous new account of causal inference, which Descartes had thought showed our rational ability to discern the "reality of the effect" within the cause. Hume saw it as simply our animal ability to learn from our experience, so to expect the future to exhibit the same regularities of temporal sequence, as we have known the past to display. It is not just an ability; it is something we cannot help doing. It is generally reliable, and indeed Hume says we would "perish and go to ruin" if we tried to stop it happening. He claims our only experience of any necessity is what we experience in our own minds when we expect a familiar effect, given that a familiar cause is known to have happened, so a rather deflating analysis of necessity in the world accompanies his account of the causal relation. This is a very important relation, since it is the one we "reason on" whenever we infer the existence of something not present to us or the occurrence of any event that we did not witness. Of course, it was also the relation that had led some thinkers to infer the existence of a God, as ultimate cause of the universe, but Hume's reasoning does not take him in that direction at all. He sticks with ordinary causes and even there argues that it is vain to expect, as Descartes had, to find the "reality" of the effect back in its cause, to find some "necessary connection" linking effect with cause. The necessity we may like to think present in the relation between cause and effect is merely a projection, Hume claims, of what we feel in causal inference: that we *must* expect the effect, given the occurrence of the cause, just as we feel that two and two *must* be four.

The "must" indicates how our minds work, not how the world is. Hume also finds that causal investigation into our beliefs about material bodies can undermine any belief that we have in the so-called secondary qualities, like color and sound, and may also undermine the belief that bodies continue to exist when unperceived. In these conclusions he is influenced both by Locke and by Berkeley. Some readers find that Hume's thesis that our minds like to "spread themselves" on the world applies not just to causal necessity but to all relations, so that space and time, too, are merely what Kant called "ideal," the contribution of our minds, not real aspects of the world. Kant did say that it was Hume who woke him from his "dogmatic slumber," but this does not mean he learned his idealism from Hume. Hume was indeed skeptical about how much we could be sure of about our world, but I think he took the relations we discern between what we know by sensation to be real, not merely projected. Indeed the "natural relations" of cause, resemblance, and contiguity are seen to influence our minds, once we have observed cases of them, and to explain the three sorts of association of our ideas. Association is the effect of our experience of the natural relations, not a primitive spontaneous proclivity of our minds. We may indeed be preprogrammed to notice some resemblances rather than others, to notice and recognize things of importance to us (such as human faces, for example), but that all such faces resemble each other in having eyes, ears, nose, and mouth, or that all circular things do resemble each other in shape, is a mind-independent fact about what resembles what. And cases of contiguity, such as the fact that eyes and nose are next to one another on the face, are taken by Hume as mind-independent facts.

Hume phrases his theory about how our minds work in terms of our "perceptions," a term Descartes and Berkeley had also used. To break down our experience into such mental units is to be a "minute philosopher," an analogue to corpuscular scientists like Boyle in the physical sciences. Locke and Berkeley were Hume's predecessors here, in taking momentary conscious states as their ultimate data, though they had called these "ideas." This puts consciousness in pride of place, since it is from its contents that all our beliefs about the world are built up. As Hume said, the science of man, and so a study of consciousness, has to be the foundation for every other science. In today's physicalist science of man, consciousness is a surd, an unexplained phenomenon, and this is ironical, if Hume is right that all our beliefs depend on it.

For Hume, perceptions come in two sorts, forcible and "original," or less lively, derivative records of earlier lively ones. The former he called "impressions," the latter "ideas," and he claimed that all our perceptions come in both forms, first as impressions, then as the cognitive content we carry away from sense experience in the form of ideas. Memory and other beliefs consist in ideas with an intermediate level of force or "vivacity," not as high as that of impressions nor as low as that of ideas of the imagination. All ideas are supposed to derive both their content and their vivacity from prior impressions, though some, like those of space and time, derive their content not directly from impressions' sense content but rather from their "manner" of appearance, the way what they present is spread out in space and time. All perceptions are "of" something and thus have "objects" or contents, which, in the case of sense impressions we take, rightly or wrongly, to present their physical causes. Our passions are also "impressions," prime examples of that life force or "vivacity" which all impressions supply and which is passed on to our volitions, and to the beliefs we form on the basis of our sense impressions. Belief in what is not present to our senses comes in the form of derivative ideas, copies of earlier impressions, which have acquired vivacity by being based on remembered past impressions and by their causal "association" with some current impression. Belief is not, as Descartes had claimed, a matter of voluntary assent but is quite involuntary. (So religious belief, or its lack, is not something one can change merely by an effort of will.)

Once this somewhat artificial construal of our conscious experience as a succession of perceptions has been made, attention has to be given to what seems to connect each perception to others in the succession. Our thought associations, or "natural relations," Hume claims, come in three variants, which select what thought follows another thought: resemblance of the objects thought about, their "contiguity" (or closeness) in space or time with each other, and the causal dependency of the object of one thought on that of its predecessor. This last relation combines contiguity with resemblance and constancy. There is no need for cause and effect in any way to resemble each other: the resemblance is between this cause and all similar past ones with the same effect, the resemblance of this effect and all those which have in the past followed the same cause. Repetition of like temporal sequences, and constancy in them (that is, that there have been no exceptions), is what leads us to confidently expect such sequences again in the future. When there has been less than constancy, we speak of probabilities. Reason cannot assure us that the future will be like the past in the regularities and frequencies displayed, or even that it is probable that it will—it is by instinct that we take this for granted. Of the three sorts of association, only causal association, based on experience of "constant conjunctions," can give us new beliefs, as distinct from recalling or fortifying beliefs we had already formed. Cause is the relation we reason on, whenever we reach a conclusion about some long past or future happening or about what is happening in a place where we at present are not.

Hume's analysis of what counts as a cause is, in his own terms, a pretty "abstruse" one. It resolves the concept of one thing bringing about or "producing" another into that of the pair of them, producer and produced, being an instance of a regular close succession, and of a regularity which we expect to continue. It seems to rule out our recognizing any sequence as a causal one the first time we encounter it, or knowing the cause of any unique effect, such as the universe. It is "skeptical" of our ability to see *why* the regular successions in our experience are as they are, or even of our chance of having rational certainty that such regularities will continue to hold good. We do not, as Descartes had claimed, discern the reality of the effect in the cause; we merely know what has regularly preceded what in our past experience. After Descartes, Leibniz had claimed that whereas animals know mere regularities, our reason enables us to see why such regularities hold. Hume denies we have such rational insight, though we may know some finer-grained regularities than other animals do. We do not know the "because" in the "cause." We do not know, Hume claims, why bread nourishes our bodies and gives us energy, but we have experience that it does. Nor does he expect that later under-standings of how bread nourishes will avoid falling back on brute constant conjunctions, though they may be different ones for the specialist than for the layman, ones of the form "first a particular enzyme encounters the bread in the stomach, then a par-ticular change takes place," allowing what we call "digestion."

Hume sums up his account of our understand-ing of causes in a double definition of cause (T 170), either as what has regularly in our experience pre-ceded its "effect," while being close or "contiguous" to it in both space and time, or, alternatively, as that, the impression of which determines our mind to ex-pect its regular follower, the "effect." He then goes on to look at "the reason of animals," the section of his book that T. H. Huxley, Darwin's disciple in the nineteenth century, found very sagacious. Hume says it is a touchstone of any species of philosophy that the account it gives of how we think and behave be extendable to animals whose behavior is similar. "No truth," Hume wrote, "appears to me more evident, than that beasts are endow'd with thought and reason, as well as men" (T 176). For beasts also learn from their experience what is likely to follow what. Their causal inferences are not, like some of ours, spelled out in language, but their basis, experience of regular successions, is the same.

Hume went on, in Part 4 of Book 1, to take several "systems" of philosophy, ancient and modern, and to subject them to a fairly skeptical survey. He also attempts some philosophy of his own, to explain why we believe that material things, and our own minds, continue to exist as the same things even when changing and when unobserved by us (in our case, in dreamless sleep). These beliefs are as regular a feature of our minds as is our faith in causal inference, and so perhaps should have been looked at in Book 3, before being subjected to skeptical survey in Book 4. For beasts, too, surely believe in lasting objects, even if they are not given to self-survey, so

Hume's "touchstone" should have been applied to his own account not just of cause but also of object-constancy. Hume, however, looks at the belief in lasting objects, and in lasting perceivers, only in Book 4. He finds both beliefs to rest on "fictions," on our minds' postulation of supposed continuants, to compensate for the episodic and interrupted nature of our experience of material bodies, including our own bodies, and of our own minds, and to "disguise the variation," especially that of our quicksilver minds, whose only interruption in consciousness is in dreamless sleep. Our perceptions must register as much variety as we take to exist, so our perceptions display maximal variation. So he ends his account of our understanding on a skeptical note. We know our own impressions and the regularities which they and their objects display. We take them to give us information about their objects and causes. We can make predictions about future impressions, based on what we believe the past has been like, and we can revise these when they prove false. We interpret our perceptions as informing us about lasting things, using interpretive "fictions" to bolster such interpretations. Beyond our impressions of it, we can know nothing about the world around us, or even about ourselves. We can know what perceptions we have had, and what regularities they have displayed, and we know what we feel and want. We regard ourselves as "persons" but can give only a poor account of what a person is. A person is a perceiver and a self-perceiver, but scarcely, as Descartes had claimed, a self-knower. George Berkeley, before Hume, had dissolved bodies into patterns of perceptions, but he thought we knew our own wills as active continuing powers. Hume's early critics, who opposed his candidature for a professorship in Edinburgh, and his nineteenth-century editor, T. H. Green, saw Hume to have reduced to absurdity the approach of Locke and Berkeley, which breaks our experience down into a series of perceptions. He had also neatly inverted Descartes' progression of thought. Descartes began in doubt and ended in certainty. Hume began with some trust in his own impressions and in his powers of thought (John Rawls calls this trust "fideism in nature") but ends Book I in an eloquent expression of despair, felt at the failure to get the hoped-for knowledge, both of world and of self. But he resolves to continue with a modest philosophical program, trying to understand the causes of our passions, the principles underlying our approvals and disapprovals, admiration and distaste, and our decisions concerning truth and falsity, reason and folly. He hopes, he says, to be

a "true sceptic" and so to be as diffident of his philosophical doubts as of his philosophical convictions.
Hume's own theories may have included dogmatic
elements, such as the postulation of distinct perceptions rather than the seamless flow we seem to experience, and there may be some dogmatism also in his
account of just what sorts of "glue" bind these elements to each other. How can he be so sure that there
are three and only three principles of association?
(Aristotle thought we also associate opposites.) There
is some tension between Hume's official skepticism
and the assurance of his own philosophy of mind.

The second book of Hume's *Treatise* is about what
he had begun by saying would be his main topic, our
passions. He begins with pride, or self-satisfaction in
our possessions, our pleasure in anything fine which
is seen as our own. This may seem a surprising place
to begin, after his conclusions in Book 1 about the
sorry fate of our intellectual pretensions and after
the difficulties he had in saying what exactly we take
ourselves to be, difficulties which seem to leave the
meaning of "my" in some doubt. But then our passions *are* "absurd," more concerned with keeping us
going than with recording truth. It is humility as
well as pride that Hume analyzes, but his main attention is to our pride in a huge range of things,

from fine cloaks to clever wit, distinguished family connections, and the climate of the place where we spent a recent vacation. He does not need to do much experimenting to know what the causes of pride are; indeed, he almost finds the reality of the effect, pleasure in ourselves as possessors, contained in its cause, pleasure in our fine possessions. The vain or unreasonably proud man, he says, automatically regards anything that is his as fine, so inverts the causal relation in pride, from "This thing is mine and pleasing, so I feel pleased with myself" to "I am pleased with myself, so everything that is mine must be pleasing." He expects most of us to have some touch of vanity. We need, it seems, to keep ourselves "in humour with ourselves," but one thing we need for that is the good opinion of others. Hume first introduces us to "sympathy," a concept very important to his version of our natures, in discussing pride in "external advantages" and in reputation. He says every pleasure languishes, unless "seconded" by the sympathy of others. So he sees us as essentially sociable, needing others as mirrors of ourselves and as confirmers of our evaluations, as well as needing some of these others as loved companions. His account of pride and its causes does not really exhibit how we must depend on observed constant conjunctions, on having noted what regularly precedes what in our experience of proud people, before we can know the causes of pride. He relies on self-analysis. And there is considerable resemblance between the cause, pleasure in fine possessions, and the effect, pleasure in oneself as possessor. Had Hume begun his *Treatise* with the passions, we might have had a quite different analysis of the causal relation.

Pride is, of course, a deadly sin for Christians, and Hume in Book 2 has Malebranche's treatment of it, in his *Search for Truth,* in fairly clear view. Some of Hume's theses echo Malebranche, for example, when he speaks of the effects on our mind of any sort of perceived grandeur. But on pride and on our love of truth, which Hume makes fun of as a sort of intellectual hunting expedition, Hume and Malebranche could scarcely disagree more. For Hume due pride is a virtue, and we can be duly proud of any virtues we possess. As Hume notes, those accustomed to the style of the pulpit will be surprised at his claims here.

Hume goes on from pride and humility to look at love and hate. Love is taken to be pleasure in the fine qualities and possessions of selected others. We move from regarding what belongs to a person as fine or pleasure-giving to regarding her as fine and pleasure-giving. (Again, the reality of the effect seems to be findable in the cause.) He gives an eloquent account of family love, though he thinks that it depends not on finding especially good qualities in our close relatives but just on our being accustomed to their company, feeling at a pleasant ease with them. Family members are familiar. That easy intimacy which he no longer had, once he moved away from home, is eloquently celebrated. When in the presence of a loved friend or relative, he writes, "the blood flows with a new tide: the heart is elevated: And the whole man acquires a vigour which he cannot command in his solitary and calm moments" (T 353). There would be many solitary and calm moments during his "country retreat" in France while he was writing his *Treatise*. He also gives an interesting account of "the amorous passion," which is taken to combine goodwill and esteem with admiration for the beloved's beauty and with lust, or "the bodily appetite for generation." The second is found to be the main ingredient in the amorous passion, since it is a medium between "the most refined passion of the soul," esteem, and "the most gross and vulgar," lust (T 395). We know very little about the young Hume's amorous passions and not much about the older Hume's. He seems to have been turned down by a young woman in Edinburgh, who later sent him a message saying that she had changed her mind. Hume's proud reply was, "So, Madam, have I." He never married, and as far as we know, and unless Agnes Galbraith is to be believed, he left no children, so any "appetite for generation" that he experienced went unsatisfied.

Other philosophers, such as Descartes, when writing about love had included love for God in their account. Hume looks at esteem for the powerful but takes this to operate partly through sympathy with the powerful person's self-satisfaction, and such an account could scarcely be extended to the case of religious people's love of God. We sympathize only with what is like us, subject to the same passions, with those whose faces we can read or whose cries we understand. Those accustomed to the style of the pulpit may be as surprised at Hume's treatment of love as at his version of pride. And any reader of Book I should be surprised at how Hume knows, without collecting empirical evidence in the form of constant conjunctions, just what the causes of pride and love must be.

The final part of Hume's account of our passions looks at the directly motivating passions of desire, aversion, fear, and hope, and he gives an intricate account of the factors that increase desire, such as postponement of satisfaction, the tantalizing veiling of the attractions of the desired, or their being forbidden fruits. (Is he here giving us a rewrite of the fall, one where Eve the temptress is veiled, not naked?) Reason serves our passions, by finding suitable objects for them, finding out the means to the satisfaction of our desires, and alerting us to the costs of such satisfaction. It cannot oppose our passions: only a passion can oppose a passion, so the traditional talk of reason and passion as opponents for control of our will depends on a misunderstanding of their nature and role. No special role is given to fear of death. Desire is for pleasure, and what is feared is pain.

In the course of his account of what determines our actions, Hume discusses the supposed liberty of the human will and finds this, our most godlike feature if Descartes is right, to be a myth. Our passions and their relative strengths, guided by our beliefs about what will satisfy them and at what cost, determine our voluntary actions, and only because we confuse ignorance of cause with absence of cause has the belief in freedom of the will come about. He thinks we are fairly good at predicting what others will do and depend on such predictions in our daily life. It is the causes of our own actions that are sometimes hidden from us, giving us "a *false sensation or experience*" of liberty. The necessity of our actions, given our motives and beliefs, is not, as Hume understands it, experienced as some irresistible force within us, but any necessity, as he had claimed in Book 1, is merely a projection of what is felt in the inference of any "thinking or intelligent being who may consider the action" and discern its causes. So when we are perplexed about the causes of our own voluntary actions, we need merely consult some observer of them. To know our own minds, we need observant companions, so that our own minds can be understood by them. Yet Hume, in la Flèche, had only his own self-inspection to go on, in delineating the human mind. Early critics found the book full of "egotisms" and said it was as if he were writing his memoirs. Yet by his own theory, each of us needs others to check our self-interpretations, and any science of human nature depends on careful observations and correct predictions based on them. So even on his own theory, worked out in solitude, the cooperative science of psychology, still in the future when he wrote, is needed if human nature is to be properly understood. He wrote to his friend Henry Home that if his views in the *Treatise* were remote from vulgar sentiments, and if accepted, they "would produce almost a total Alteration in Philosophy" (NL 3). But he later granted that his book was useful not so much for the truths it contained as for the questions raised and the hints given. It did contain many general truths about human nature, because its self-inspecting author's nature was in most respects typical, and it did raise important questions about the source of our confidence that the future would resemble the past in its regularities, about the causal relation, about our ideas and the world around us, and also about our range of motivation and the role of reason in directing conduct. Hume is happy to speak of reason as a director, as long as it is clear that our aims are set by our passions. Reason directs us so as to get what we most want.

Book 2 can be read as a thoroughgoing correction of the puritan Christian moral psychology Hume had been taught, according to which pride is a sin, and many natural desires are also sinful, in need of control by some higher God-given faculty, such as reason or conscience. If Hume is right, it is counterproductive to label natural desires "sinful." To issue lists of prohibitions is simply to make their recipients curious about what pleasures the forbidder is trying to prevent them from sampling. "The notion of duty, when opposite to the passions, is seldom able to overcome them, and when it fails of that effect, is apt rather to increase them" (T 421).

In the third book of the *Treatise*, *Of Morals* (published a year after the first two, along with an appendix making some comments on the theses of the first book, in particular on belief in general, and on our belief in our own personal identity), Hume looks at the source of our moral approbations (approvals) and finds that it is a special sympathy-dependent sentiment that decides which character traits in one another we welcome and approve of. Morality, in the form of a "catalogue of virtues," is the outcome of such sentiments. This makes morality depend not, as many of his predecessors had held, on what God demands of us but on what we ourselves find acceptable and praiseworthy. A large part of Hume's attention is given to the virtue he calls "justice," namely, the willingness to conform to society-relative rules decreeing who has a right to what. His Book 2 conclusions about the dangers of too many disciplinary rules are at work here, and the rules of "justice," as he understands them, are a minimal set and are basically enabling rules, not straight prohibitions. They result from informal agreements between people in one place, when they see a common interest in observing these rules. Hume called this sort of agreement a "convention," and his account of it has been much praised by later game theorists. The "circumstances of justice" are scarcity of wanted resources, along with our limited willingness to share with each other. Hume sees us not as egoists concerned only with our selves but as concerned also for family and friends, as having what he termed "limited generosity." In these circumstances, our ancestors were intelligent enough to see that it would be in all their interests to accept restrictions on "the heedless and impetuous" expression of their desire for possessions. In what John Rawls, in his *Lectures on the History of Moral Philosophy,* calls a wonderful part of Hume's text, Hume writes of what he thought would have been the first convention, that establishing property rights:

> This convention . . . is only a general sense of common interest; which sense all the members of the society express to one another, and which induces them to regulate their conduct by certain rules. I observe, that it would be in my interest to leave another in possession of his goods, *provided* he will act in the same manner with regard to me. He is sensible of a like interest in the regulation of his conduct. When this common sense of interest is mutually express'd, and known to both, it produces a suitable resolution and behaviour. And this may

> properly enough be called a convention or
> agreement betwixt us, tho' without the interpo-
> sition of a promise; since the actions of each
> of us have a reference to those of the other,
> and are perform'd upon the supposition that
> something is to be performed on the other
> part. (T 490)

Wonderful indeed this passage is, and deservedly admired. Once property rights have been invented, there
follow conventions for voluntarily transferring them
from one person to another, by gift or by barter, then
by promise and contract, which enable us to transfer
future or distant goods or services. The rules of justice tell us what counts as our property and tells us
we must respect others' property rights; they show us
how to make a promise, as well as telling us that we
must keep it. There is no prohibition on taking what
is in another's possession, only on taking his property, whether or not it is currently in his possession.
There is no prohibition on changing one's mind, or
on not doing what one said one would do, only on
going back on one's word. Both property and promise enable us to do things that we could not without
them. Only with property rights are we able we have
security of possession, warranted trust that most

people will not remove what is in our possession. Only with contractual rights are we able to count on others doing what they have solemnly sworn they will do, when this affects our own plans and interests. Promise and contract extend trust, Hume says, beyond family and friends to strangers, though some basic trust in one another is shown in acceptance of any convention, when we trust others to conform to it. Hume sees our ancestors to have "invented" property, promise, and (later) governors. Of course, once they are invented, there will indeed be new prohibitions, such as "Don't steal, don't break contracts," just as the enabling rules of a game generate some forbidden moves or fouls. As nothing would count as a double fault at tennis without the enabling rules of the game, so nothing would count as theft unless property rights are being recognized. Since it is local "convention" which determines the details of property rights, and the details of what counts as a valid contract, Hume calls this virtue "artificial," dependent on social "artifices," but he emphasizes how natural it is for human communities to have such informal agreements on cooperative schemes, allocating rights to individual persons. It is property and promissory rights he concentrates on, and he believes these would have been in effect before the special job of magistrate was created, to declare and enforce such rights. Before magistrates, these conventions were taken to be self-enforcing, as long as there was a common interest served by them. Only in large societies where disapproval of theft and fraud is insufficient to prevent them, or where offenders can move on to those who do not know of their past offenses, are magistrates needed.

The last social artifice Hume discusses is marriage, which he takes to be what enables children to get the care of both their parents and enables parents to be able to count on each other for their lifetimes, though it is only the wife's sexual fidelity which is essential to marriage's main purpose, as Hume sees it, since he thinks fathers need assurance that the children they help care for are really their own. Reading Hume's sardonic account of marriage makes us understand why he avoided it, especially as he found divorce to be against the interests of the children of the marriage. As he put in a later essay, "Of Polygamy and Divorces," the possibility of divorce would put "it in the power of parents, upon every caprice, to render their posterity miserable" (Ess 188). But as he had earlier conceded, without that possibility, marriage can become a prison. In his account, the point of marriage was not to express the amorous passion, nor even "solid and sincere amity," but to provide for the proper rearing, by both parents, of their children. Hume expected the amorous passion for a particular person never to last long and thought that marriage is best built on the more lasting foundation of common interest and sober friendship. Of the social artifices Hume discusses, marriage for life, with chastity expected only of the wife, is the one he described most negatively. Any such artifice is supposed to be for the advantage of "the whole and every part" of society, but it is difficult to see that either adult women or adult men do benefit from the arrangement Hume describes. Plato's communal crèches seem benign, in comparison, as a way of getting children properly cared for, during what he termed their "long and helpless infancy." It is during this time that children learn to speak and learn the customs of their group, and so become acculturated. Later ethologists have seen this long infancy, or "serious prematurity of birth," as what explains our possession of a much richer culture than other species exhibit. Birds may learn birdsongs, and cats are taught by their mothers to bury their fecal excreta and how to hunt, but we learn far more while in our malleable prolonged childhood. It is best if children have both parents to care for them and to initiate them into their culture, but Hume knew from his own experience that a child brought up by one parent need not be disadvantaged. Or did he feel his father's absence so strongly?

Although magistrates enforce the right not to suffer assault, in addition to property, promissory, and marital rights, Hume says little about it, if indeed he saw it as a right. He never speaks of natural rights. He usually speaks of rights only when some social artifice has recognized them. He regards gentleness as a virtue, cruelty as the most detested vice, and apparently sees no agreement or "artifice" to be needed for us to tell what counts as assault and as cruelty, whereas we do need to appeal to local agreement as to what is whose property, in order to know what counts as theft or breach of contract or as adultery. (Sometimes we do also need positive law to determine when smacking children counts as assault.) Hume calls virtues "natural" when, unlike justice, they can show themselves whatever the local customs, but he does not see their recognition as giving rise to rights. Such natural virtues include benevolence, generosity, gratitude, parental solicitude, kindness, courage, proper pride, modesty, frugality, industry, cheerfulness, serenity, patience, perseverance, and abilities such as foresight, wit, eloquence, and good sense. Hume knows that some moralists deny merit to involuntary abilities such as good sense, but he sees no reason not to include all valued traits in his list of virtues. He is realistic about what we do admire and deplore in one another and rightly says that no one wants to be thought stupid. So stupidity counts as a vice, just as much as cruelty or dishonesty. The decision as to moral merit is not, for him, as it is for religious moralists, a prelude to reward and punishment, unless approval and disapproval themselves count as that. He sees such reactions to the character of those around us to be involuntary and inevitable, not, like reward and punishment, deliberate attempts to show our pleasure and displeasure. Being the object of involuntary distaste may be hurtful, but it is not suffering deliberate punishment.

The first part of Book 3 of the *Treatise* had been devoted to the question of what role reason plays in moral judgment. Here Hume applies what he had argued for in Book 2. Reason can work out the effects of actions and habits of action, but the decision as to whether such effects are welcome is made by our capacity to feel pleasure or distress, when this is influenced by our capacity to share others' pleasure and distress. We do not need any special "moral sense" or "conscience"; our sense of what is admirable and contemptible and our capacity for sympathy are enough to explain our moral judgments. Hume repeats his earlier claims about the role of reason to serve our passions and the need for such lively passions to motivate action. If morals are to affect action, he claims, they must engage our passions. The sentiment that counts as moral approbation, however, is a faint one compared with such strong passions as self-interest, so disapprobation alone is rarely enough to deter action, especially if Hume is right that forbidden fruits have a special relish for us. In the case of justice, he claimed that only the interested passion can control the interested passion, so it is only when we see that our greater interest lies in keeping society's rules that we are likely to respect them. Wise approbations will be for traits that occur quite naturally, like parental solicitude, and for forms of self-interest that also serve common interests. There is no point in disapproving of human nature—the wise moral judge will select for approbation the best versions of human motives and abilities, ones which it is not too difficult for us to display. Hume says that we always consider "the *natural* and *usual* force of the passions, when we determine concerning vice and virtue" (T 483), and treat as vice anything that departs, on either side, from the human norm. This is a little in tension with his claim that we take pride in our virtues and so see them as in some way better than the norm. We will naturally admire most, in one another, extreme degrees of virtues, such as courage, generosity, and patience, and also displays of any degree of any virtue in very difficult conditions.

Hume concludes his *Treatise* with the claim that his version of morals has the advantage of showing how it arises from a "noble source," namely, our capacity for sharing good and ills, through sympathy, and acting for the common good. It is "extensive sympathy with mankind," not any need to placate gods or demons, which is the source of Hume's version of morals, and he believes that a better understanding of our own nature will serve to improve our understanding of human morality and the content it should have. Here again he is revising biblical stories, especially the version of morality of the hellfire preachers, who regard its dictates as those of a jealous and vengeful god, who first creates us sinners, then forbids us what we naturally want. The whole of the *Treatise* challenged Christian teaching about our nature, that we are a special creation with a special destiny and a duty to crucify our sinful flesh. For Hume we are intelligent talking animals, who share with the other higher animals our passions, capacity for sympathy, and ability to learn from experience.

Unlike them, we can share our individual experience with those with whom we can talk, and we have a fortunate capacity to invent social schemes of co-operation, as well as wheels, looms, spinning jennies, and printing presses, but we have in addition a deplorable propensity to imagine gods, to bow down before them in fear and adoration. It was not until his "Natural History of Religion," published in 1757, that Hume looked closely at this last human specialty, but those zealots who opposed his candidacy in 1745 to the Edinburgh chair of moral philosophy had clearly appreciated the *Treatise* for the irreligious work it is.

Hume added an appendix to the *Treatise* when he published Book 3. In it he clarifies his theory of belief and expresses doubts about Book 1's account of our belief in our own identities. He seems to see a tension between his claim that each of our perceptions is distinct from the others, without any necessary connection with them, and his claim that the associative relations within the series of one person's perceptions are enough to produce the belief that such a series constitutes one personal history. He says he is involved in a "labyrinth," and Hume scholars delight in mapping this labyrinth but do not agree on exactly what was worrying Hume. It is true that he had presented our conscious experience as if it came in the form of discrete separable bits, which he called "perceptions," rather than as a continuing stream, and that his associationist or connectionist account of what relates these atoms to each other may be inadequate to restore continuity to what he had somewhat artificially precipitated out from the flow of experience. Mental association explains why a given thought calls up another thought but not what impression follows another impression, and there are, of course, impressions as well as ideas in what he calls the "bundle of perceptions" which make up a person. Association may explain why some memory of past experience evokes a connected memory but can scarcely explain the temporal order of the life which is remembered. Is this what worried Hume? He had allowed that the content of our ideas of space and time arose not from any impression of them but from the "manner" in which our perceptions come, spread out in space, when they are sense impressions, and in a temporal sequence. Perhaps they also come, for each person, in a personal manner, as mine not yours. This would not make them necessarily connected with each other but would explain what meaning we give to "my" when we speak of "my perceptions." (Marina Frasca Spada has a book, *Space and the Self in Hume's Treatise,* about these various manners in which Hume thinks our perceptions come.) Hume never returns to this topic in his later writings, so we cannot know of any second thoughts he had. Or should we take his account of his own life, which I am using to introduce my chapters, as a late return to the question of what holds a life together?

Did Hume's first readers realize how revolutionary was his version of our nature? He was by no means the first in a Christian culture to discard the doctrine of original sin, but earlier thinkers who had done so, such as the Cambridge Platonists, had not attempted a full naturalistic account of our nature, as Hume does. "The most abstract speculations concerning human nature, however cold and unentertaining, become subservient to *practical morality;* and may render this latter science more correct in its precepts, and more perswasive [*sic*] in its exhortations" (T 621). Hume revises both the content of practical morality and his culture's understanding of the human mind and person. He allows some place in our minds for deductive reason but sees most of our beliefs as depending more on induction and on our habits of mental association. Present-day connectionists in cognitive science and believers in neural networks can look back to Hume, and his talk of our thought "rummaging the neighboring cells" in the brain, as founding hero. And Jerry Fodor, with his representationalist theory of mind, sees his own views as *Humean Variations* (the title of one of his books). But Hume's first readers did on the whole find his abstract speculations on human nature cold and unentertaining, and he was bitterly disappointed at the reception that his *Treatise* received from reviewers and at its low sales. He had expected it "to excite a murmur among the zealots" and was disappointed that, apart from a review or two, it was at first ignored. He later said he had gone to press too quickly and should have taken more time for revision and perhaps also for some abbreviation of the lengthier stretches of reasoning. He believed the "principles" the work contained were sound but that there were some "negligences in reasoning, and more in the expression." Later readers delight in pronouncing on just where these negligences are to be found and have refused to do what Hume requested: to look only to his later writings for his considered views. These did make his animus against religion more unmistakable. But his first work had a young person's daring and breadth of scope, and his later restatements of his main theses are often enlivened and clarified when read against their first and more elaborate formulations. His *Treatise* remains most of his admirers' favorite Hume work, despite its author's later disclaimers about its merits. And since T. H. Huxley hailed the work as a revolutionary account of our nature and its relation to that of other animals, the "sagacity" of Hume's unrelenting naturalism has been more consistently recognized. Huxley wrote that Hume's *Treatise,* composed before its author was 25, "is probably the most remarkable philosophical work, both intrinsically and in its effects on the course of thought, that has ever been written." That Hume asked us not to read it is ironic. But he gave it and its reception more space in *My Own Life* than he did any of the works he hoped we would read. He had said in its pages that we especially desire "what is forbid," so his request that we not read it could have been a calculated tease.

3

HUME AFTER THE *TREATISE*

In 1742 I printed in Edinburgh the first part of my essays: the work was favourably received, and soon made me entirely forget my former disappointment. I continued with my mother and brother in the country, and in that time recovered the knowledge of the Greek language, which I had too much neglected in my early youth.

In 1745 I received a letter from the Marquis of Annandale, inviting me to come and live with him in England: I found also that friends and family of the young nobleman were desirous of putting him under my care and direction, for the state of his mind and health required it. I lived with him a twelvemonth. My appointments during that time made a considerable accession to my small fortune. I then received an invitation from General St Clair to attend him as Secretary to his expedition, which was first meant against Canada, but ended in an incursion on the coast of France. Next year, to wit 1747, I received an invitation from the General to attend him in the same station in his military embassy to the courts of Vienna and Turin. I there wore the uniform of an officer, and was introduced in these courts as aid-de-camp to the general, along with Sir Harry Erskine and Captain Grant, now General Grant. These two years were almost the only interruption which my studies have received in the course of my life: I passed them very agreeably, and in good company; and my appointments, with my frugality, had made me reach a fortune which I called independent, though most of my friends were inclined to smile when I said so; in short I was now master of near a thousand Pound.

I had always entertained a notion, that my want of success in publishing the Treatise of Human Nature, *had proceeded more from the manner than the matter, and that I had been guilty of a very usual indiscretion, in going to the press too early. I, therefore, cast the first part of that work anew in the* Enquiry concerning Human Understanding, *which was published while I was in Turin. But this piece was at first but little more successful than the* Treatise of Human Nature. *On my return from Italy, I had the mortification to find all England in a ferment, on account of Dr Middleton's* Free Enquiry, *while my performance was entirely overlooked and neglected. A new edition, which had been published in London of my* Essays, moral and political, *met not with a much better reception.*

Such is the force of natural temper that these disappointments made little of no impression on me. I went down in

1749, and lived two years with my brother at his country house, for my mother was now dead. I there composed the second part of my Essays, *which I called* Political Discourses, *and also my* Enquiry concerning the Principles of Morals, *which is another part of my* Treatise *that I cast anew. Meanwhile my bookseller A. Millar, informed me that my former publications (all but the unfortunate* Treatise*) were beginning to be the subject of conversation, and that new editions were demanded. Answers by Reverends and Right Reverends, came out two or three in a year, and I found, by Dr Warburton's railing, that the books were beginning to be esteemed in good company. However I had fixed a resolution, which I inflexibly maintained, never to reply to any body, and not being very irascible in my temper, I have easily kept myself clear of all literary squabbles. These symptoms of a rising reputation gave me encouragement, as I was ever more disposed to see the favorable than the unfavorable side of things, a turn of mind which it is more happy to possess, than to be born to an estate of ten thousand a year.*

In 1751, I removed from the country to the town, the true scene for a man of letters. In 1752, were published at Edinburgh, where I then lived, my Political Discourses, *the only work of mine that was successful on the first publication. It was well received abroad and at home. In the same year was published at London, my* Enquiry concerning the

Principles of Morals; *which, in my own opinion, (who ought not to judge) is of all my writings, historical, philosophical, or literary, incomparably the best. It came unnoticed and unobserved into the world.*

After what he saw as the failure of his abstruse philosophy to find any significant readership, Hume seems to have resolved to try to write in a more accessible style, and he published essays designed for a wide readership, on topics ranging from the freedom of the press and eloquence, to delicacy of taste and passion, from national character and the rise and progress of the arts and sciences to marriage and divorce. Some of these essays try to emulate Addison and Steele and to appeal to a female readership. He later withdrew these somewhat condescending essays as "frivolous" and dubious in tone. There were also some political essays, about the party system in Britain, about civil liberty, and, prophetic for his later look at Cromwell's commonwealth, on "whether the British government inclines more to Absolute Monarchy, or to a Republick." Then there are four essays portraying four species of temperament found in philosophers, in those who take themselves to be Platonists, Epicureans, Stoics, or skeptics. The last and longest of these four essays is often taken as a presen-

David Hume, from an unsigned portrait, reproduced by kind permission of the Ross family of Edinburgh, in whose home it has hung since its purchase from the Earl of Stair c. 1930 by Mr. S. K. Ross, a descendant of Hume's nephew, Baron Hume.

tation of Hume's own outlook, since he often called himself a skeptic. Of these early essays, one that was important for Hume's later themes is "Of Superstition and Enthusiasm," in which Catholic and Protestant temperaments are contrasted, ready for Hume's look at the roles these two opposing Christian religions had played in English history, and also ready for Hume's more general look at superstition and religious belief in his "Natural History of Religion." The essays on eloquence and delicacy of taste prepare the way for his later dissertation, "Of the Standard of Taste." These early essays, which did cover the sort of topics Hume would have dealt with had his *Treatise* been extended, as first planned, by two more books, were fairly well received.

But Hume had not given up hope of making the claims of his three *Treatise* books more palatable to a thoughtful readership, so, during an unhappy year as tutor to the mentally unbalanced Marquess of Annandale, and after his unsuccessful bid for a chair of philosophy in Edinburgh, he began "recasting" each of the *Treatise*'s three books in three shorter works. *Essays* (later *Enquiry*) *Concerning Human Understanding* was published in 1748 while Hume was in Turin, as secretary to his distant cousin, General St Clair, with whom he spent two years on a military embassy at the end of the War of the Austrian Succession, implementing the peace terms agreed to by Vienna, Turin, and Sardinia. (England had supported Austria against Prussia, France, and Spain in this war. Indeed, England was at war with France for much of Hume's adult life, but he managed two lengthy stays in France during the periods between these wars.) Next to be published was his recasting of Book 3 of the *Treatise, An Enquiry Concerning the Principles of Morals* in 1751, and last, "Of the Passions," a much reduced version of Book 2 of the *Treatise,* which was one of the *Four Dissertations* he published in 1757. The other three dissertations were the mischievous and quite offensive "Natural History of Religion," the shorter "Of Tragedy," and the much admired "Of the Standard of Taste," which explains some disagreement on what is good literature by our varying versions of what is agreeable, some by the ignorance or insensitivity of the judges. He also wrote very successful essays on politics and economics, published in 1752, and these were quite quickly translated into French.

The first book of the *Treatise* was recast into the considerably different *Essays* [later *Enquiry*] *Concerning Human Understanding* while Hume was a tutor at Weld Hall in 1745, where he probably also rewrote the second book of the *Treatise,* in "A Dissertation of [later "on"] the Passions." It was also during that year in England that he applied for the chair of philosophy at Edinburgh and wrote his anonymous "Letter from a Gentlemen to His Friend in Edinburgh," sent to Provost Coutts, but edited and published by Henry Home (later Lord Kames), to counter some of the claims about his *Treatise* that were being made by those who opposed his candidature. He had already published an "Abstract" of the *Treatise,* concentrating mainly on its first book, in particular on the analysis of what we take a cause to be. It also stressed the account of association, which runs through all three books. The charges answered in the anonymous published pamphlet largely concern the views presented in its first book, but the whole work had been charged with "sapping the foundations of morality." This was linked with what was seen as atheism and a denial of the immateriality of the soul. Hume's skepticism comes under attack, as does his reduction of our experience, indeed of our minds themselves, to a series of perceptions. His account of how our causal inferences depend on the regularities we have observed was thought to ground these skeptical and anti-religious conclusions, since Hume's view of what we mean by a cause does seem to rule out any first cause. As he argued in his *Enquiry Concerning Human Understanding,* we would need to have experience of some constant conjunction between universes and their causes to have any idea of what might have caused this universe. What Hume and Home do in the letter is quote the charges, then deny that Hume himself had drawn the atheistic and materialist conclusions attributed to him. Strictly speaking, this is right, but nevertheless there is something a little less than candid about the letter, just as there is something less than balanced about the "Abstract" of the *Treatise.* Hume, or his friends, are of course right to complain of those who give *"Maim'd Excerpts"* and "broken and partial citations" from a long work, picking sentences out of context in order to make their charges. It is even claimed in Hume's letter that the argument for God's existence, from the apparent design of the universe, gets strength from his account of causal inference, as depending on our experience of natural constancies, such as that between beautiful buildings and the "Design and Contrivance" of clever architects.

Hume, when he wrote this letter to Coutts, was already at work on his first *Enquiry,* which contained two sections fairly openly attacking the foundations of Christian belief, in Section 10, "Of Miracles," and, attacking any theism, in Section 11, "Of Providence and a Future State," in which he has Epicurus look at what can reasonably be inferred about the creator from "the visible phenomena of the universe." In the latter, after Epicurus has had his say, Hume points out that we really have no grounds for forming any belief at all about the cause or causes of a *unique* effect, the world, since we need *regularities* of sequence to get evidence of causes. Epicurus is made to say that if we do postulate such a cause of the world, it must have only the features needed to explain its known effect, the world as it is. We could not attribute goodness and justice to the world's supposed creator, unless we do think we find "distributive" justice in the world. What the religious do, Epicurus says, is invent a future life to make up for the injustices in this world, but this is sheer fantasy, wishful thinking. Hume would soon begin working on his *Dialogues on Natural Religion,* in which the "argument from design," the claim that this world is splendid enough to justify us in taking its creator to be great and good, is subjected to fairly merciless attack, so it was disingenuous of Hume or his supporters, in the gentlemanly letter, to pretend that the author of the *Treatise* supports this argument. Technically it is correct to say it is not there attacked. It is faintly possible that the first version of the *Treatise,* before Hume "castrated it of its nobler parts" before letting Bishop Butler see it, did contain some reference to the design argument, perhaps after his account of analogy there, so he may have felt bitter at having cut it out and having been accused of atheism anyway. His attacks on the argument from design were not published till after his death, since his friends thought they would give too much offense, but one thing they might also have feared was that readers of the *Dialogues* would remember what had been said in the not really so gentlemanly published letter. It took six years for Hume's *Treatise* to excite the murmurs among the zealots that he says he had expected, but he does not seem to have appreciated them once they came.

Should we regret that Hume failed to become a philosophy professor? Although he got on well with young people, it is difficult to imagine him as an educator of young Scots, many of them intended for the professions of law and the church. His lack of a solemn professorial manner is part of what appeals in his writing, and he would have had to resort to great hypocrisy to subscribe to the Westminster Confession of Faith. What he did instead, become a military secretary after the end of the War of the Austrian Succession, enabled him to see more of Europe and gave him the worldly experience that informs his later essays. His letters back to his brother about his travels with General St Clair are a delight. Travel, he tells him, is the best cure for prejudice. He is impressed with the fertility of the Rhine Valley and goes by ship down the Danube to Vienna, where he tells how Maria Theresia was afraid he and other members of their party would fall over themselves in trying to leave her presence without turning their backs on her, so excused them from the formal mode of departure. Vienna struck him as small, for a capital, and he makes fun of the attempt to evict all "loose women" from it, to the "Frontiers of Hungary, where they can only debauch Turks and Infidels" (L 1:128). The number of people in Styria suffering from thyroid problems and other deformities is commented on, and he seems to have found the Germans more impressive in health and well-being than the Austrians. He even makes the following conjecture about the southern route from Vienna, "the great Road thro which all the barbarians made their Irruptions into the Roman Empire": "they always left there the Refuse of their Armies before they entered the Enemy's Country." Hume wonders whether "from thence the present inhabitants are descended. Their dress is scarce European as their figures are scarce human."

Carinthia, though pretty, is no better, as far as its inhabitants go. Once in South Tirol, however, the "aspect of the people is wonderfully chang'd, . . . an Air of Humanity, & Spirit, & Plenty is seen in every face: yet their Country is wilder than Stiria" (L 1:131). Once in Italy, Hume kisses the soil of Mantua, which produced Virgil, but finds it a beggarly and miserable town. His long letter to his brother ends as they approach Turin, where they are to stay a while. Just what he did in Turin, other than serve his general, write letters for him, read Montesquieu, and pay his clumsy respects to a young married woman who cruelly had another admirer watching behind a screen (James Cauldfeild, Lord Charlemont, who left us a rather malicious account of the occasion) we do not yet know, but some Italian scholars (Emilio Mazza and Edoardi Piccoli) are currently looking into that.

How does his recasting of Book 1 of the *Treatise* in the first *Enquiry* differ from the original? Hume puts back in some of the explicitly anti-religious content he had left out of the *Treatise* and leaves out any account of our belief in our own identity, most of the detail about how we get our ideas of time and space and about how we come to make the causal inferences and probability estimates that we do. The most important differences, as I see the matter (and other

Hume readers may stress other changes), are the greater acknowledgement that we do pool information, by "books and conversation," and therefore do accept what scientists tell us are the laws of nature as long as they do not contradict what we think our own experience has shown us; changes to his account of how we form our beliefs; and changes to his definitions of what we take a cause to be. Changes in the double definition of cause include the elimination of the requirement that causes be close in space and time to their effects and the elimination of any reference to "impressions" of the cause or effect. This is not because Hume has ceased contrasting vivacious impressions with less vivacious ideas but because he has altered his theory of belief, which had, in the *Treatise,* required a current impression, or at least a memory impression, to supply vivacity to any idea which comes to be believed. Most belief formation, if not from indoctrination and testimony, is from observation, memory, and causal inference, so his *Enquiry* account of how we get new beliefs from our causal inferences was affected by his doubts about his *Treatise* theory of vivacity-transfer, an account that his early reviewers had ridiculed. There was also a problem in finding any impressions of the mental causes which his theory had taken to be real.

There had, I think, been an embarrassing incoherence in the original *Treatise* story, although since many of his readers have not seen it, I may be mistaken in finding it there. None of his causal claims about our minds, their perceptions, and those perceptions' causal interrelations were covered by his original definitions of what we take a cause to be, since perception-causes do not have spatial position, and we do not have sense-impressions *of* them. The new definitions allow for mental causes, which are of course the main ones in which Hume, as scientist of the mind, is interested. The science of the mind, in the first *Enquiry*, becomes more of a collaborative enterprise, and the definitions it works with allow for its own findings, as well as allowing for action at a distance. This may be an advance, but Hume the scientist of the mind just backs away from the topics, such as belief in personal identity, that had daunted him before.

Nothing is said in the first *Enquiry* about our self-conceptions, and all our belief-forming habits are simply said to be due to inexplicable instinct. We in a sense become more like the other animals, in this revised account of how we proceed—all of us depend on cognitive instincts, though ours are extended and complicated by our ability to read and talk, do science, and to judge the worth of one another's testimony. One topic Hume did develop a little was that of the supposed liberty of the human will. To his *Treatise* claim that our actions are predictable, caused by our passions and beliefs, Hume adds that any blame for bad outcomes always switches to any will (such as that of a hypnotist) behind a given human will, so any creator-god may be seen as responsible for the evil we do, if God made us the way we are and foresaw our decisions and their consequences. This may be one of the overtly anti-religious bits Hume had cut out of the *Treatise,* and it does give extra bite to his discussion of liberty and necessity. Some of Hume readers hail this *Enquiry* as a work of great enlightenment. Others of us, while welcoming the noble parts possibly excised from the *Treatise,* prefer the latter—omissions, faults, and all. Hume requested that readers ignore the *Treatise* and concentrate on the later works, but his request has been regularly ignored. Even admirers of the *Enquiry* want to go back to the *Treatise,* to compare and contrast.

Hume's recasting of Book 2, in his "Dissertation on the Passions," cuts out much of what had made the original account provocative and interesting, and has not been not much attended to. The one interesting addition it makes is the claim, at the end, that

Hume hopes to have shown that "in the production and conduct of the passions, there is a certain regular mechanism, which is susceptible of as accurate a disquisition, as the laws of motion, optics, or any part of natural philosophy." This repeats what Spinoza had said in the preface to his treatment of the human affects, in Book 3 of his *Ethics,* that "the affects, considered in themselves, follow with the same necessity and force of nature as the other singular things.... I shall consider human actions and appetites just as if it were a question of lines, planes and bodies." Both Hume and Spinoza, like Hobbes before them, were determinists, who took all of human behavior to be predictable, and Hume's account of the details of our passions repeats much of what these predecessors had written, with some points from Malebranche added, so was not very original. Where Hume differs from Spinoza is in giving the passions the role of commander, while reason is mere intelligence service. Here Hume agrees with Hobbes.

The recasting of Book 3, "Of Morals," in *An Enquiry Concerning the Principles of Morals,* has to do without the psychological background that Book 2 had provided for Book 3 of the *Treatise* and is, I think, the worse for that. Hume wrote it when he was back at home in Ninewells, with his sister and brother, after he returned from his army service a little richer, "master of near a thousand pounds," and maybe a little wiser in the ways of the world. (His mother had died during his time in England, and his grief at her death was deep.) This second *Enquiry* was published in 1751, and Hume declared it to be incomparably the best of all his publications. Of course, Hume's judgment has prompted his readers to wonder just why this work was what he, in a letter to the Abbé Le Blanc, called "my favourite performance." It is much more polished than Book 3 of the *Treatise* and much richer in examples of human virtues and vices, most of the examples taken from historians. It avoids the offensive term "artificial" when speaking of justice, but the substance of his earlier account of justice as requiring the adoption of "conventions," or social schemes of cooperation, and conformity to them, remains in place. Hume adds a discussion of the "sensible knave" who breaks the rules of justice when he thinks he can get away with it, while hoping others will not do the same. Such a knave may gain in riches but at the cost of secrecy about his actions and of any sense of integrity. If he does not mind that, then there is no way the moralist can reason with him. Marriage, and breach of its rules, is discussed only in passing, when female chastity is again listed as a virtue made necessary by "the long and helpless infancy of man," which requires "the combination of the parents for the subsistence of the young, and that combination requires the virtue of chastity or fidelity to the marriage bed" (E 206–207). He goes on to make clear that this is expected of wives, not husbands, and that such a virtue would never have been dreamed of, but for its utility in assuring husbands of their biological fatherhood of their wives' children.) Hume's contemporary, James Balfour, a lawyer who became professor of moral philosophy in Edinburgh, was very upset by these claims about the mere utility of female chastity.

There is no longer a fuss made, in *An Enquiry Concerning the Principles of Morals,* about the limits of reason's role in morals: all virtues are approved either for their agreeability or their utility to their possessors or others, and for judging utility, reason has a vital role to play in working out consequences. So although it is taste or sentiment that pronounces the final judgment as to which character traits are virtues, fact-finding and much reasoning have to pave the way. This is indeed quite different, and much less shocking, than the *Treatise* claims about reason being slave to the passions and impotent to motivate action. But there was still plenty to shock the religious.

The "monkish virtues" of "celibacy, fasting, penance, mortification, self denial, humility, silence, solitude," are transferred to the column of the vices, since they "stupify the understanding and harden the heart, obscure the fancy and sour of the temper" (E 270). James Balfour was outraged by such claims, by the treatment of chastity, and by the fact that Hume kept, in this work, the *Treatise* analogy of moral virtues to advantages of the body, especially to sexual attractiveness, and counted personal charm as a moral virtue. Indeed, Balfour wrote a book, *A Delineation of the Nature and Obligation of Morality,* to counter what he saw as Hume's pernicious influence. Both Balfour and after him Adam Smith thought that Hume underestimated the importance of "self-command" and disagreed with his view that the distinction between what we can and cannot help is of little moral importance, that virtues include involuntary as well as voluntary abilities. What we could and could not have helped is important for deciding when we merit punishment, but, if Hume is right, not for deciding whether our character is to be admired or to be deplored. Hume does present a fairly Epicurean non-moralistic version of how we appraise each other, and by his emphasis on increased human happiness as the point of morality, he inspired Bentham and later Utilitarians.

There is a contrast between Hume's two *Enquiries* in how he chose to end them. The first ends in a challenge to us to burn all books which contain neither mathematics nor "experimental reasoning," though it is fairly obvious that it itself does not pass this test. But in the second *Enquiry,* even in his "Conclusion" (before the four appendices that follow) Hume had fallen back into "diffidence and scepticism" about his own claims that we can agree about what character traits are admirable, since "men still dispute concerning the foundation of their moral duties." This continuing disagreement is then enacted in "A Dialogue," tacked on as a final word on Hume's part. There the human record of disagreement on such topics as suicide, infanticide, homosexuality, and adultery is canvassed, and the last word is a warning against philosophical "enthusiasm." So this really is a carefully crafted work, which is skeptical in that it puts both sides of a case and leaves the matter undecided. That it still outraged Balfour and Beattie, and did not really please Adam Smith, shows how entrenched were the teachings of Calvin and Knox in Hume's culture. His having freed himself from them is a sort of miracle—how did he do it? He was already free of Puritan scruples, except concerning willful waste, when he wrote the *Treatise,* so it can scarcely have been the effect on him of foreign and less Puritan cultures. He continued to the end to pride himself on his early "frugality," but his essay "Refinement in the Arts" was originally titled "Of Luxury" and points out the economic and cultural benefits of some consumer pleasures. Something in his early life made him a cautious hedonist, and his ethics are as fine an example as we have of how morals need not be killjoy, nor wear a "dismal dress," but can, and if enlightened will, produce "a greater happiness."

Hume says his *Political Discourses,* published in 1752, were "the only work of mine that was successful on the first publication." These included not merely his essays on luxury, on the party system in Britain, the two essays on obedience to governments, one called "The Protestant Succession," a slightly surprising one titled "The Idea of a Perfect Commonwealth," a very learned essay on population, and the remarkable "Some Remarkable Customs," but also his essays on money, on interest and credit, on trade, and on tax, all of which were important contributions to economics and influential for Adam Smith. "Some Remarkable Customs" picks on customs that seem to go against principles accepted in the nations where they were to be found. One is the practice that Athens and Thebes had of prosecuting those who proposed a law which was accepted but proved bad for the public. As Hume points out, this might seem to threaten freedom of speech in debate but was a good control on demagoguery. Some of Demosthenes' most eloquent speeches were given in the special court where such charges were laid. The next remarkable custom is the Roman one of having two separate assemblies which could enact laws, that of the centurions and that of the tribunes. For long this worked well, and it wasn't until the time of Mark Antony that its provisions were abused, by calling on the tribunes to rule on one of the few matters, appointment of governors to provinces, which was reserved for one assembly only, in this case for the centurions. The third remarkable custom was the right of the British Crown to have press gangs to "impress" (that is, to forcibly conscript) men to be seamen, though in other matters Parliament had to supply the Crown with what it sought, in the way of taxes or service. This, in fact, was one of the continuing customs that incited the American colonies to rebel. Hume supposes it to continue, despite its obvious violation of the liberty of Englishmen, since no other way of supplying the navy had been found (conscription for military service lay well in the future, first briefly tried during the French Revolution). But Hume praises Hampden, who refused to pay his ship money tax, and notes that supplying ships and supplying those to work them should, on the face of it, both have been parliamentary matters, not monarchical powers. Hume finds it remarkable that in England Hampden was a hero for refusing to pay ship money, when Charles I levied it without Parliament's consent, but the impressing of seamen to man those ships went on without any parliamentary protest, so presumably with their tacit consent. And remarkable it indeed was. But this joint custom, of refusing the Crown money for the Royal Navy, but allowing the Crown to kidnap young men and force them into labor at sea, is unlike the other two Hume considered in the essay, in that although it may serve to supply a navy, it was not exactly working well, at least not for the young men forced to go to sea. Was Hume trying to stop the practice? This is a remarkable essay, and its point is a little mysterious. Daniel Defoe in 1728 wrote a pamphlet about the impressing of seamen and was definitely against it. Among other disadvantages, he says it delayed the departure of warships in times of emergency, while they waited for press gangs to return with their haul of new seamen. The practice began with Edward I, was made legal under Elizabeth, provoked increasing outcry during the eighteenth century, and was finally ended in 1814, after Napoleon had been defeated. Hume says at the start of his essay that he wants to show how difficult it is in politics to establish any firm principles which do not have exceptions, since irregularities seem to abound, and some things in fact work quite well which seem, on the face of it, doomed to failure. Each of the three cases he took involve an apparent inconsistency: the Greeks wishing to have free debate in legislative assemblies, along with their custom of prosecuting those whose oratory led to the adoption of what were later deemed to have been bad laws; the authority of an assembly to pass laws for the Roman republic, despite a competing different assembly having the same authority; and the British Crown's need to get Parliament's consent to tax citizens, including taxes to build ships, and the Crown's being allowed to impress seamen to man those ships in time of war. The cry of the American rebels was "no taxation without representation!" But in fact it was the press gangs, as well as taxation, which led to their rebellion. Hume's perhaps prophetic question was "why make a rule for taxation but not for forced labor, for ships but not for the seamen to man them?" If his essay, "Of the Idea of a Perfect Commonwealth," looks back to Cromwell's commonwealth, his "Of Some Remarkable Customs" looks forward to the abolition of impressing seamen, forty years after his death.

What, you may well ask, of those worse cases of forced labor, namely, the practice of slavery and the whole feudal system, which expected peasants to fight for their lords? Hume discussed ancient slavery in "Of the Populousness of Ancient Nations," and also in *An Enquiry Concerning the Principles of Morals,* in tones of unmistakable horror at its cruelty and oppression. In fact, when he was employed in a sugar-importing firm in Bristol, the likelihood is that its ships, on the westward journey, took African slaves to America or the West Indies. I like to think that this was one reason Hume did not last long there, but there is no evidence to support this conjecture, except Hume's later words about slavery. There is an apparently racist footnote to his essay "Of National Characters" in which he says he knows of no cases of dark-skinned people having shown any talent in the arts and sciences. He had within the essay wondered whether climate might affect national character but had thought "moral" causes, such as imitation of our fellow countrymen, more important. He certainly does not suggest that the more "civilized" should make slaves of others, whatever the color of their respective skins and whatever their ability or lack of it.

The abolition of slavery had to wait much longer than the abolition of the practice of impressing seamen. Feudal practices were discussed in his *History,* once he got back to the medieval period, for Hume wrote his history backward, as it were, attending first to the century closest to his own before going back to Tudor times, then to the medieval period.

Religion was clearly very much on Hume's mind in this decade. It is directly discussed in one of his early essays, "Of Superstition and Enthusiasm," where Catholics are given the main share of superstition, that is, belief in the magic of ritual and prayers to statues, while Protestants show religious "enthusiasm," or belief in their own divine inspiration. Some Protestant protest against superstition may be "furious and violent," but it may, Hume believes, in the end be more conducive than superstition to liberty of opinion. This essay discusses only variants of the Christian religion, but Hume casts his net more widely in his "Natural History of Religion," on which he was working during this time. It was not published until 1757, as one of *Four Dissertations,* along with "Of the Passions" (a partial rewrite of Book 2 of the *Treatise*), and dissertations on tragedy and "Of the Standard of Taste." In this last he considers varying judgments on the worth of literary works, explaining this largely by the difference in the knowledge and sensitivity of different critics and the different cultures in which the judgments are made. The dissertation on religion associates monotheism with the furious spirit of enthusiasm, while Catholic Christianity is treated as virtually polytheistic, and there are offensive jokes about how many gods there are, given that several divine persons are prayed to and gods are regularly eaten by the faithful in the Mass. There was also an offensive footnote to his essay "Of National Characters" saying that hypocrisy is the occupational vice of clergymen, whatever the brand of religion they served. Then there is also a passing mention in "Of the Protestant Succession" of the inquisitors, stakes, and gibbets that have attended Catholic monarchs, so, even if polytheistic, Catholic Christianity can show a very intolerant face. The essay "Idea of a Perfect Commonwealth" includes in its vision a "Presbyterian" established religion, tolerant of all bishop-free sects and controlled by a state-appointed council of religion. Hume hoped for increasing religious toleration but is cautious. "Though it is much to be hoped" he writes in "Of the Protestant Succession," "that the progress of reason will, by degrees, abate the acrimony of opposite religions all over Europe, yet the spirit of moderation has, as

yet, made too slow advances to be entirely trusted"
(Ess 510).

These various essays and the "Natural History of
Religion" make it understandable why, when Hume
began his *History of England* a little later, it was with
the seventeenth century that he chose to begin. The
English civil war was a religious as well as a political
war, part of the "acrimony of opposite religions all
over Europe," and it was natural that Hume would
want to look closely at it. The Gunpowder Plot, the
contest between Archbishop Laud and the Puritans,
Hampden's protest over ship money, the details of
Cromwell's commonwealth—all these matters would
make him want to look closely at the early Stuarts,
at the fall of the English monarchy under Charles I,
and at "the triumph of the saints."

4

HUME AS LIBRARIAN
AND HISTORIAN

In 1752, the Faculty of Advocates chose me as their Librarian, an office from which I received little or no emolument, but which gave me command of a large library. I then formed the plan of writing the History of England; but being frightened with the notion of continuing a narrative through a period of 1700 years, I commenced with the accession of the House of Stuart, an epoch when, I thought, the misrepresentations of faction began chiefly to take place. I was, I own, sanguine in my expectations of the success of this work. I thought I was the only historian, that had at once neglected present power, interest, and authority, and the cry of popular prejudices; and as the subject was suited to every capacity, I expected proportional applause. But miserable was my disappointment: I was assailed by one cry of reproach, disapprobation, and even detestation: English, Scotch, and Irish, Whig and Tory, churchman and sectary, freethinker and religionist, united in their rage against the man, who had presumed to shed a generous tear for the fate of Charles I, and the Earl of Strafford; and after the first ebullitions of this Fury were over, what is still more mortifying, the book seemed to sink into oblivion. Mr Millar told me, that in a twelvemonth he sold only forty five copies of it. I scarcely, indeed heard of one man in the three kingdoms, considerable for rank or letters, that could abide the book. I must only except the primate of England, Dr Herring, and the primate of Ireland, Dr Stone, which seemed two odd exceptions. These dignified prelates separately sent me messages not to be discouraged.

I was, however, I confess, discouraged; and had not war been at the time breaking out between France and England, I had certainly retired to some provincial town, have changed my name, and never more returned to my native country. But as this scheme was not now practicable, and the subsequent volume was considerably advanced, I resolved to pick up courage and persevere.

In this interval I published at London my Natural History of Religion, *along with some other small pieces: its public entry was rather obscure, except only that Dr Hurd wrote a pamphlet against it, with all the illiberal petulance arrogance, and scurrility which distinguishes the Warburtian school. This pamphlet gave me some consolation for the otherwise indifferent reception of my performance.*

In 1756, two years after the fall of the first volume, was published the second volume of my History, *containing the period from the death of Charles I, till the Revolution. This volume happened to give less displeasure to the Whigs, and was better received. It not only rose itself, but helped to buoy up its unfortunate brother.*

But though I had been taught by experience, that the Whig party were in possession of bestowing all places, both in the state and in literature, I was so little inclined to yield to their senseless clamour, that in above a hundred altera-tions, which further study, reading, or reflection engaged me to make in the reign of the first two Stuarts, I made all of them invariably to the Tory side. It is ridiculous to con-sider the English constitution before that period as a regular plan of liberty.

In 1759 I published my History of the House of Tudor. *The clamour against this performance was almost equal to that against the History of the first two Stuarts. The reign of Elizabeth was particularly obnoxious. But I was now callous against the expression of public folly, and continued very peaceably and contentedly in my retreat in Edinburgh, to finish, in two volumes, the more early part of the English His-tory, which I gave to the public in 1761 with tolerable, and but tolerable, success.*

Once his brother married, Hume had moved, with his sister, from Ninewells to Edinburgh in 1751. They at first lived in Riddle's Close, at the top of the Royal

James Court, Edinburgh, where Hume moved in 1762, although
the buildings as photographed here are altered since Hume's
day, and today are completely rebuilt into luxury apartments.
Photographed by the author in 1986.

Mile, near where he had been born, and later moved to Jack's Land. In 1752 he was appointed librarian to the Faculty of Advocates, so had "command of a large library. I then formed the plan of writing the History of England." Letters written when he was accepting the post as secretary to General St Clair suggest that he had formed that plan considerably earlier and had thought that travel would help equip him to write his *History*. "Town," he says, is "the true scene for a man of letters," and these years in Edinburgh were very busy and sociable ones for him. He and his sister, with the help of their faithful servant, Peggy Irvine, entertained their many friends, including the rather humorless professor of rhetoric Hugh Blair, the talkative historian William Robertson, and the more reserved and solemn Highlander Adam Ferguson, whose *Essay on Civil Society* Hume at first feared might be found to contain some Highland barbarisms. (It in fact gave an alternative conjectural history of human customs to that Hume himself had given, in Book 3 of the *Treatise,* one that plausibly mapped social progress on the shifts from pastoral to agricultural, then to manufacturing ways of life.) He had a lively correspondence both with fellow Scots (with his old friends Gilbert Elliott and William Mure, and with Adam Smith, Allan Ramsay, and with John

Clephane, on the use of "enow" and "enough") and with Montesquieu, Le Blanc, and Rousseau in France. His historical research engrossed him, and one book he hoped to get from David Dalrymple was a biography of Cromwell, called *Flagellum*. It was a scurrilous life of Cromwell, first published in 1663, and Dalrymple replied to Hume's inquiry by telling him there was no need to cite Julian the Apostate's views on loaning, especially since Hume was "happax photizomenos," which in New Testament Greek means "once baptized." (It can also, in classical Greek, mean "once enlightened.") Hume's treatment of Cromwell is fairly judicious and balanced. (He does not cite the book he had asked Dalrymple for, citing Whitelocke and Thurloe to balance the royalist bias of Clarendon.) He had chosen the accession of the house of Stuart as his entry point into British history, since it was "an epoch when, I thought, the misrepresentations of faction began chiefly to take place." Hume wrote history in order to understand the present. In his *Treatise* he had devoted two long sections in Book 2 to the influence on our imagination of distance in space and time, especially time. He says there that it is easier to go back a short than a long distance, as we continually revert to the present, so have to let our mind go to and fro between past and present, somehow representing in our thought all the intervening period between, say 1603, when James assumed the throne, and 1752 or 1753, when Hume was writing about James.

The beginning of the reign of James VI of Scotland—and as James I of England—was a natural place for a Scot to begin a history of Britain, since it saw the union of the crowns, the official entrance of Scotland into the kingdom of Great Britain. Once one does go back in time, the historian will then relate events in the order they occurred, so Hume progresses from the Gunpowder Plot through to the civil war and the beheading of Charles I, then the rule of Cromwell and the Restoration. Then in the next volume, published in 1756, he takes us through the reigns of the later Stuarts, eventually bringing his readers up to 1688. *My Own Life* tells us that he was "frightened with the notion of continuing a narrative of 1700 years" so first went back only modestly far in time, nevertheless to a time of religious divisions which it was difficult to speak about with impartiality, and the on to the civil war, which had left lasting animosities in English society. He had tried to avoid biased representations, but when the first volume appeared, "I was assailed by one cry of reproach, disapprobation, and even detestation: English, Scotch,

Irish, Whig and Tory, churchman and sectary, free-thinker and religionist, patriot and courtier, united in their rage against the man who had presumed to shed a generous tear for the fate of Charles I and the Earl of Strafford." One would think that sectaries and patriots would be more likely to disapprove of this generous tear than courtiers and churchmen, and certainly Hume had shed no such tear for the fate of Oliver Cromwell and his family after the Restoration. (Cromwell was disinterred and posthumously beheaded, but Hume does not mention this final indignity.)

Between his history of the Stuarts and that of the Tudors, his next dip back into the past, Hume himself suffered the indignity of being accused, along with Henry Home (by now Lord Kames), of infidelity and immorality, by a group in Edinburgh, who brought their charges in 1755 and 1756. They were headed by a former army chaplain, George Anderson, whom Hume, in a letter to the painter Allan Ramsay, described as "the godly, spiteful, pious, splenetic, charitable, unrelenting, meek, persecuting, Christian, inhuman, peace-making, furious Anderson." Anderson had published his "Estimate of the Profit and Loss of Religion" in 1753, and John Stewart had earlier called Hume's orthodoxy into question. There is little doubt that

Hume was an infidel, but he had exercised some caution in what he had published, at least before the "Natural History of Religion," and certainly had not been guilty of any known "immorality" beyond pointing out, in his "Dialogue" appended to the *Enquiry Concerning the Principles of Morals,* how adultery was tolerated in the France of his time. He had tried, in 1751, to publish his mischievous "The Bellman's Petition," making fun of pleas for higher salaries for the clergy, but the printers had refused to publish it. In 1755 his friends among the moderates in the Edinburgh clergy rallied in his support, and the charges against Hume and Kames were dropped, muted into a general resolution deploring the appearance in Scotland of books encouraging immorality. One of Hume's wittiest critics was John Witherspoon, who went on to become president of Princeton and who had published an analysis of "The Character of a Moderate Man," one of whose claims was that "when any man is charged with loose practices, or tendencies to immorality, he is to be screened and protected as much as possible" by moderate men. These moderates included Hume's professor friends Hugh Blair and William Robertson as well as the young lawyer Alexander Wedderburn, and they did indeed do their best to screen and protect Hume and Kames. Hume does not tell us about this episode in *My Own Life*. Quite a bit is censored out of it, including the two main charges of infidelity, the failures to get a professorship of philosophy in Scotland, and his reprimand, when librarian in Edinburgh, for ordering obscene books. Hume's friends had quite a lot to smooth over for him.

Writing his Tudor history required Hume to spend time in London consulting state papers. He had in any case resigned from his job as librarian in Edinburgh after a reprimand for ordering books deemed unsuitable for the library, including *L'Histoire amoureuse des Gaules* by Bussy-Rabutin. (Dalrymple was one of those who reprimanded him.) Just as Hume had wanted to illuminate the Hanoverian era by seeing how the Stuart period had led up to it, so he wanted to understand the state of the monarchy which James I inherited and the overstepping of royal powers that Charles I was thought guilty of. The key to that lay in the long reign of Elizabeth, so Hume went back to the Tudors, claiming in several letters that he wished he had chosen to begin there. To his good friend Dr. John Clephane he wrote in September 1757:

> I am now very busily engaged in writing another volume of History, having crept backwards to the reign of Henry VII. I wish, indeed, that I had

begun there: For by that means, I should have
been able, without making any digression, by the
plain course of narration, to have shown how
absolute the authority was which the English
kings then possessed and that the Stuarts did
little or nothing more than continue matters in
the former tract, which the people were determined no longer to admit. By this means I
should have escaped the reproach of the terrible
ism of them all, that of Jacobitism. (L 1:264)

(He had earlier in the letter complained that Clephane
had joined with "the great multitude who abused me,
and reproached me with Paganism, and Jacobitism,
and many other wretched *isms*.") Once his research
turned to the reign of Elizabeth, Hume was in frequent contact with William Robertson, who was writing a history of Scotland, to make sure they shared
what information they had about Mary, Queen of
Scots, a very controversial topic. That Hume saw
Robertson not as a rival but as a fellow historian
comes out very clearly in this correspondence, though
Robertson's attitude to him was less cooperative.
They did not agree on all matters, and it is interesting that it is the relation of Mary to her son, James I,
that they most disagreed on. Hume saw James as a

dutiful son to a bad mother, while Robertson saw him as a bad son to a not-so-bad mother. Hume had wanted to get clear about James's past, since he had begun his own history with that king's reign. To know that James's mother had threatened him with disinheritance of the right to the crown of Scotland if he did not become a Catholic, and that, despite that, he had supported her against Elizabeth, was important for Hume for understanding James. He made many corrections to that part of his Stuart history, not only as he went forward to the later Stuarts, but even more when he went back in time, to what had prepared the ground for James I's rule.

Among the letters we have from this period in Hume's life is a very amusing one, dated July 6, 1759, from London, where he was working on his history, to William Rouet, professor of church and civil history at Glasgow, a cousin of William Mure, and a friend of the two Misses Elliot with whom Hume was staying (L 1:309–311). Rouet had asked one of them to ask Hume for news from London, so Hume gives him a bulletin of it, all false and facetious. Seven French ships had been sunk by Admiral Hawke, and the young Prince Edward had lost both legs in the engagement. Despite this setback, the French had landed a large invasion force in Torbay, producing panic in London, but there was no will to resist, rather resignation to "the French, Popery and the Pretender." Pitt has been sent to the Tower for treason. Warburton (who had protested against Hume's "Natural History of Religion" and himself written *The Divine Legation of Moses*) had turned Mahometan, been circumcised, and was busy on the divine legation of Mahomet. Hume writes that he saw Warburton in the Mall wearing his turban, which became him very well. Printer Andrew Millar (known for his parsimoniousness) has been declared bankrupt, and Miss Anne Elliot, one of two respectable spinster sisters, with whom Hume lodged, has turned out to be a bigamist, with two secret marriages, while her sister, Miss Peggy Elliot, is in correspondence with three gallants. Some of Hume's humor, such as the young prince's lost legs, is in questionable taste, but the jokes about Pitt, Warburton, and the Misses Elliott show a fine strain of satire. Most of Hume's preserved correspondence from this period is serious in nature: letters to Millar and Strahan about his own publications, to Robertson about Mary, Queen of Scots, to Kames about the views of the economist Tucker, several letters to the Abbé Le Blanc in France, who had translated Hume's *Political Discourses* and whom Hume hoped might translate his Stuart history. In April 1759 there is a teasing letter to Adam Smith about the reception in London of Smith's *Theory of the Moral Sentiments,* in which he pretends that he is constantly interrupted, before giving Smith the news of the enthusiastic reception the book was receiving (NL 51–55). In 1761 Hume writes his first letters to Hippolyte de Saujon, the Comtesse de Bouffleurs-Rouverel, who had written to him praising the "divine impartiality" of his first Stuart volume, and the next year Hume writes to Jean-Jacques Rousseau, a friend of the Comtesse, telling him that, since the death of Montesquieu, "you are the Person whom I most revere, both for the Force of your Genius and the Greatness of your Mind." His letters to the Comtesse are of extreme courteousness, that to Rousseau also very respectful, so that the joking letters to Rouet and Smith come as a relief after these. Asked by the Comtesse about his opinion of Rousseau's *Emile,* Hume praises the eloquence and says the work carries the stamp of great genius, but also says that Rousseau has "scorned to dissemble his contempt of established opinions" so should not be surprised at being persecuted by the authorities in Switzerland. Hume writes to Thomas Reid, whose *Inquiry into the Human Mind* he had been shown by Hugh Blair, and in which Hume finds a few Scotticisms ("hinder to" instead of "hinder from"). He kindly points these out while praising the work for its combination of deeply philosophical content and spirited expression. There are also letters to Horace Walpole, about whom Hume had published an essay, later withdrawn, and to Benjamin Franklin.

The last part of his history to be written was from the Roman invasion up till Henry VII. Hume was reputed to have written these volumes from a divan, and he showed less interest in this period than in Britain's later history. He certainly did not exert himself to search for overlooked documents. But it was these volumes which, when translated into Italian, got the whole work put on the Index. He was very scathing in his treatment of Becket (H 1:336) and indeed of the role of the church throughout most of the medieval period. Henry II was one of the monarchs Hume most admired, and so Hume smooths over the king's role in the death of Becket and plays up both his wisdom in protecting Jewish money lenders and his wise legal reforms, one of which made murder a capital crime. (Earlier murder had been treated either as theft of manpower, punished with a fine, the size of which depended on the sex and rank of the victim, or as breach of the king's peace.) Hume treats the introduction of Christianity to Britain as an improvement over the "barbarity" of the Saxon religion, as much for the contacts it brought with southern Europe as for any particular features of that religion. By the time of Queen Elgiva, in the tenth century, the church's rules had become despotic and cruel. Hume describes in horror the punishment (hamstringing) inflicted on her for marrying her cousin, King Edwy (H 1:95). He had earlier found Henry VIII's assumption of right to decree church doctrine arrogant and dictatorial, but the fates of Edwy and Elgiva, at the hands of the church, gets an indignation on Hume's part matched, in his *History*, only by that shown at the fate of Charles I from the Puritan Parliament. Other kings like Edgar the Martyr and Edward II had been horribly killed, and several queens were beheaded, but not by religious fanatics. Adam Potkay has described these volumes of the early history of England as a supplement to Jonathan Swift's *Gulliver's Travels,* in particular Gulliver's account, told to the head horse of the Houyhnhnmns, about the absurd matters of disagreement which had led to bloodshed and quarrel. But indeed the whole history, not just the medieval volumes, is a diagnosis of the causes of quarrel and war, and in particular of the role of religion in that. It was only with the Reformation that quarrels about Christian doctrine rent Europe, but earlier heretics and offenders against church law had been persecuted, and the Crusades had pitted Christian against Muslim. Hume deemed them the worst folly the human race had displayed. (In some ways this was prophetic on his part of the current strife between some Western countries and the Muslim world.)

Hume's *History* traces mainly changes in government, law, and social institutions, including the church but also glances at trade, at social customs such as diet, and also at the literature and science of the various periods. Milton and Newton get the highest praise, despite their religion and Milton's republican sentiments. Shakespeare is criticized for lack of refinement. Hume had written an essay called Tthe Rise and Progress of the Arts and Sciences" and saw such cultural development as not independent of economic and political progress, and cultural progress as going along with technological. He dwells in his *History* on the transformation to life that the printing press brought (H 3:140). Burton rightly said of Hume's *History* that "he was the first to add to a mere narrative of events, an enquiry into the progress of the people, and of their arts, literature, manners, and general social condition." Burton deplores what he sees as Hume's lack of appreciation for the likes of Pym and Hamden and his supposed lack of knowledge of the English constitution, and Burton links this with Hume's failure to study law long enough and the restriction of his study to Justinian and the Civil Law. But as Ritchie had pointed out, in his earlier biography, Hume's early study of that law, however superficial, "gave a bias to his studies, which, being seconded by favorable events, suggested, at a future period, the project of compiling his *History:* a task which he undertook, not from a wish to detail battles, and exhibit a tedious succession of political broils, but for the more dignified purpose of tracing the progress of legislation and civility." Hume surely does, as Ritchie says, want in his *History* to trace the development of the English constitution, in addition to tracing, as Burton says, the general social and cultural condition of the English people. Both these aims were included by Hume in his description of the appeal of history, in his early essay, "Of the Study of History." "What more agreeable entertainment . . . than to observe human society, in its infancy, making the first faint essays towards the arts and sciences, to see the policy of government, and the conversation of civility refining by degrees" (Ess 565–566).

5

HUME'S LIFE AS A MAN
IN THE PUBLIC EYE

But, notwithstanding this variety of winds and seasons, to which my writings had been exposed, they had still been making such advances, that the copy money given me by the booksellers, much exceeded anything formerly known in England; I was become not only independent, but opulent. I retired to my native country of Scotland, determined never more to set foot out of it; and retaining the satisfaction of never having preferred a request to one great man, or even making advances of friendship to any of them. As I was now turned fifty, I thought of passing the rest of my life in this philosophical manner, when I received, in 1763, an invitation from Lord Hertford, with whom I was not in the least acquainted, to attend him on his embassy to Paris, with a near prospect of being appointed secretary to the embassy; and, in the meanwhile of performing the functions of that office. This offer, however inviting, I at first declined, both because I was reluctant to begin connexions with the great, and because I was afraid that the civilities and gay company of Paris, would prove disagreeable to a person of my age and humour; but on his lordship's repeating the invitation, I accepted it. I have every reason, both of pleasure and interest, to think myself happy in my connexions with that nobleman, as well as afterwards with his brother, General Conway.

Those who have not seen the strange Effect of modes, will never imagine the reception I met at Paris, from men and women of all ranks and stations. The more I recoiled from their excessive civilities, the more I was loaded with them. There is, however, a real satisfaction in living in Paris, from the great number of sensible, knowing, and polite company with which the city abounds above all places in the universe. I thought once of settling there for life.

I was appointed secretary to the embassy; and in summer 1765, Lord Hertford left me, being appointed Lord Lieutenant of Ireland. I was chargé d'affaires *till the arrival of the Duke of Richmond, towards the end of the year. In the beginning of 1766 I left Paris, and the next summer went to Edinburgh, with the same view as formerly, of burying myself in a philosophical retreat. I returned to that place, not richer, but with much more money, and a much larger income, by means of Lord Hertford's friendship, than I left it and I was desirous of seeing what superfluity could produce, as I had formerly made an experiment of a competency. But, in 1767, I received from Mr Conway an invitation to be Under-secretary; and this invitation, both from the character*

of the person, and my connexions with Lord Hertford, pre-
vented me from declining.

In 1763 Hume was invited by Lord Hertford to act as
his secretary at the Paris embassy. At first Hume de-

David Hume, by Charles-Nicolas Cochin le jeune, c. 1754.
Credit: Harvard Art Museums, Fogg Art Museum, Gift of
Forsyth Wickes, 1962.150. Allan Macintyre © President and
Fellows of Harvard College.

clined, "because I was reluctant to begin connections with the great, and because I was afraid the civilities and gay company of Paris, would prove disagreeable to a person of my age and humour." He was 50 and seemed to think that an age to "retire to my native country of Scotland." He had in fact expressed an intermittent wish to live in France and certainly seemed to enjoy his time there once Lord Hertford prevailed on him to accept the embassy position. He was "loaded with civilities," and the Anglophile Hippolyte de Saujon, Comtesse de Bouffleurs, with whom Hume had earlier been in correspondence, made him very welcome once she had recovered from the measles which afflicted her on his arrival in Paris. She made sure that he was received in all the best salons. As a royal mistress, her own social position, though high, was not quite what Hume had been accustomed to among his women friends in London and Scotland. She addressed him as "Cher Maitre," even when chiding him for taking too long to reply to her recent fulsome letter, expressing "une amitié que mon coeur ressent si vivement" (a friendship which my heart feels so strongly). It is not surprising that Hume found these self-obsessed and effusive letters from a royal mistress difficult to reply to, however flattering her attentions may have been. She made it quite clear to him that she hoped to become a princess, hoped, that is, that the Prince de Conti would marry her after the death of her husband, so her affair with Hume was only a dalliance and a tease. Hume tried to gently suggest to her that the prince was unlikely to marry again, but she persisted in her vain hopes. Hume does not seem to have been sorry to leave France when the time came. In the month of his own death, August 1776, he wrote the Comtesse a letter of condolence on the death of the Prince de Conti, telling her ("dear madam") that his own death was fast approaching and that he had no anxiety or regret. "I salute you, with great affection, and regard, for the last time." Among the things he presumably did not regret was his return to Britain, rather than accepting her and the prince's offer of an apartment in their grand quarters in the Temple, Paris, with a view into their garden, where they would be "trés proches, l'un de l'autre" (very close to each other). He seems not to have wanted that degree of closeness. She wrote to him in May 1766 that the apartment was ready, comfortably and prettily furnished and with "une bibliotèque suffisante, et si vous ne travailler pas, ce sera votre faute" (an adequate library, so that if you do not work, it will be your fault). But he was no one's tame philosopher, writing to order, nor anyone's kept man. He boasted of not having wealthy patrons, to whom his books would have to be dedicated. He valued his independence above all. Clearly Madame Bouffleurs did not mind being a kept woman, and it does seem very generous of the Prince de Conti to offer Hume the desirable apartment. Was it because he foresaw that he would not continue writing that he was reluctant to be set up in the Temple as a writer-in-residence? At any rate he declined the offer, and his literary efforts after his Paris stay were restricted to corrections, mainly to his *History* but also to his *Enquiry Concerning the Principles of Morals,* whose last correction was made in his last year of life.

Hume seems to have quickly become a favorite in Paris, if also slightly ridiculed for his heavily Scots-accented French and his clumsy manner. It was his writings that brought him acclaim in France, and of course he was pleased about that. The most famous story of his time with the philosophes and Encyclopedistes is that he said, at a dinner party with the Baron d'Holbach, that he was yet to meet a genuine atheist. The baron told him there were seventeen around his dining table at that moment. What had Hume meant? He knew that his French friends were not religious believers, any more than he was. The Prince de Conti, his lady love's protector, like Hume himself was a skeptic but not an atheist. Hume was not certain there was no God; he just saw no good enough reason to suppose that there was. And he thought all reasonable people would have the same detached and undogmatic attitude. But among his new French friends he found a more confident surety, when it came to irreligion. It was not wholly to his taste as a true skeptic.

Hume seems to me to have been an innocent abroad during his second French sojourn, though some see his time there as the high point of his life and his affair with Hippolyte de Saujon as a deep romance. I do not see his time in Paris this way. He was not up to the cynicism or opportunism of his lady love, nor really at home among the Paris atheists. The exceptions were the editors of that compendium of enlightenment, the twenty-seven-volume *Encyclopedie,* namely, Denis Diderot, whose first publication was on what the sighted can learn from the blind; and the learned mathematician and translator of Tacitus, Jean le Rond d'Alembert, whose origins were as a foundling on the steps of the church of Jean le Rond, then in an orphanage, and to whom Hume left two hundred pounds in his will. (D'Alembert's natural father in fact paid for his education and left him in fair financial shape. Diderot, in contrast, had been disinherited by his family and imprisoned for anti-religious writings but had received the patronage of Catherine II of Russia, when she heard that he was selling his large library to get a dowry for his daughter. Catherine bought it, left it with him, paid him a salary as her librarian, and at his death the books went to Russia.) Both the fashionable aristocrats and these savants were enchanted with Hume, partly for his innocence when combined with the wisdom of his writings. In a way he had more in common with Rousseau, also ill at ease among the fashionable Parisians. Both of them were like wild children, when plonked into the company of such basically depraved persons as the Comtesse de Bouffleurs, who condemned royal mistresses like Madame de Pompadour while being little better herself. That Hume did not see through her pretensions amazes me. Perhaps in the end he did. She had begun by flattering him, and he was not accustomed to flattery. He did briefly succumb and enjoyed her company. He seemed to have no premonitions, while in Paris, that in a mere thirty years the guillotine would be employed to behead the royal Bourbon prince who had received him so graciously at Versailles and Fontainbleau, and that many of his acquaintances would have to flee for their lives. (The aging Hippolyte de Saujon was arrested during the Terror but acquitted.) What Hume would have made of the French Revolution is unclear. Horror at its violence and bloodthirstiness, certainly, but what of the cry for equality? He had shown little sympathy for that when it had been expressed by the Roundheads. In his *Enquiry Concerning the Principles of Morals,* he had said that the cost of trying to maintain any approximation to an admittedly desirable economic equality would be "rigorous inquisition" and "severe jurisdiction," leading to tyranny. But he did show understanding of outrage felt at extreme disparity in wealth, for social conditions in which a rich man's satisfaction of "a frivolous vanity frequently costs more than bread for many families, or even provinces." He did not seem to have had any sense of just how rotten the support in France for its ancien régime had become, nor of the level of popular outrage at inequality and at the conspicuous consumption of royalty and aristocrats and their pampered mistresses.

It was to please Hippolyte de Saujon that Hume agreed to accompany Rousseau back to England when he left Paris. She, if Rousseau is to be believed, had made improper advances to the French philosopher, which he repulsed, but she wanted to help him and so had enlisted Hume to help him get safely to England, when Rousseau was being persecuted in Switzerland. This Hume did and found him a refuge in Derbyshire. But poor Rousseau became convinced that Hume had been mocking him and so turned against Hume, making wild accusations. He provoked Hume into what I regard as his least creditable publication, his "Concise Account" of his dealings with Rousseau, one work he does not mention in *My Own Life*. It was published first in French, since in a sense it was written for Hume's Paris acquaintances and with their encouragement. I find the whole matter, from start to finish, a sort of unkind joke on the part of Hume's supposed friends in Paris, who set him out on his journey with the paranoiac Rousseau, took part in the public mockery of Rousseau in England, and relished Hume's indignant protest of innocence. It was a sort of philosophers' comic opera, and both philosophers were demeaned by it. His Edinburgh friends tried in vain to stop Hume rushing into print, but Hume knew Rousseau was writing his memoirs, so feared that he would suffer calumny in them. (In fact, it was Hume's false lady love whom Rousseau singled out for unfavorable mention.)

Hume was not only loaded with civilities in Paris; he was also, I think, somewhat mocked. His inadequate French (related by Madame d'Epinay in her account in a letter of how Hume played the part of a sultan in some charade, flanked by two young beauties, over whom he could only stutter, "Mes cheres demoiselles, mes cheres demoiselles!") his crimson-suited bulk, his clumsiness, and his disarming gaze all singled him out as a sort of court fool. "Le bon David" maybe, but he needed all his good nature not to feel somewhat laughed at while in Paris. Maybe he reacted as strongly as he did to Rousseau's accusations precisely because he did know how mockery can hurt. He never returned to France after his duties were ended and seemed relieved to be back in Britain, where he knew his way around better, both in London where he spent eleven months as undersecretary of state, assisting General Conway with relations with nations in northern Europe, and even more so in Edinburgh, where he went, with a government pension, in 1769 and where he ended his days. His smart Parisian dress on his arrival back in England was reported later by a member of the Cauldfeild family, who as a 5-year-old child had been impressed by "the philosopher's uncouth ponderous person, equipped in a bright yellow coat, spotted with black." Unfortunately, none of his portraits show him in this coat, though the ones we have display very fancy coats and waistcoats. Maybe it was chosen for him by Madame Bouffleurs, as a change from the embassy red outfit?

The political scene in London while Hume served first the Rockingham government, then the government of Grafton, was that commented on in the *Letters of Junius,* published in those years. The mysterious Junius found great corruption there. Lord Bute was living with the widowed queen mother, Agatha, in Kew, and caused much anti-Scotland feeling. It was not an easy time for a Scot to be in any sort of charge of affairs of state. The Wilkes populist riots were already brewing. Hume saw much of Lord Hertford and General Conway and their families and does not seem to have found his duties irksome or arduous. He was able to help some of his Edinburgh friends, Blair and Robertson, since relations with Scotland, as well as European nations north of France, came within his responsibilities as assistant to Conway. He was glad when he could return to his Edinburgh friends. He seems to have had no salary for his government work, though some perks came his way, but he did receive a government pension at the end of his service. He described this service as that of "a philosopher, degenerated into a petty statesman."

While Hume was in London, the Douglas cause was the hot legal topic. After the death of the first Duke of Douglas, the vast estate was claimed both by spokesmen for the young Duke of Hamilton, a cousin of the duke, and for Archibald, the son of the sister of the deceased duke, whom the Hamilton camp claimed was not really her biological son, since she was 51 when she supposedly gave birth, in Paris, to twin boys (one of whom later died). In Edinburgh, the Court of Session had decided in favor of Hamilton; then the decision was appealed to the House of Lords in London, who reversed it and awarded the estate to Archibald Douglas. Hume's good friend Baron Mure was one of Hamilton's guardians, so it was natural that Hume should support Hamilton, and Hume was outraged at the decision against him and at Lord Mansfield, who delivered it. Boswell took the other side in the dispute, which he wrote about. He believed that the principle of "filiation" was at stake, that a child should be able to believe what its parents tell it about its parentage, not have its status as their child challenged. Hume, who had been in Paris while the Hamilton supporters gathered evidence about the possible purchase by Lady Jane Douglas of newborn baby boys, apparently believed that no woman of 51 could possibly give birth for the first time, and that the fact that the child had been brought up by her as a member of the Douglas family counted for little against Hamilton's undisputed blood tie. It seems a strange matter for Hume to have become so concerned about, whether a cousin or a supposed nephew should get the Douglas inheritance, but maybe part of Hume's indignation was that a court in London could overturn what the Court of Session in Edinburgh had decided. For once in his life, he and Bishop Warburton, who had written against Hume when his "Natural History of Religion" had appeared ten years earlier, were of one mind, in questioning Lord Mansfield's "propensity for Douglas."

6

HUME'S FINAL YEARS
IN EDINBURGH

I RETURNED TO EDINBURGH in 1769, very opulent (for I possessed a revenue of 1000 pounds a year), healthy, and though somewhat stricken in years, with the prospect of enjoying long my ease, and of seeing the increase of my reputation.

In spring 1775, I was struck with a disorder in my bowels, which at first gave me no alarm, but has since, as I apprehend it, become mortal and incurable. I now reckon on a speedy dissolution. I have suffered very little pain from my disorder, and what is more strange, have, notwithstanding the great decline of my person, never suffered a moment's abatement of my spirits; insomuch, that were I to name a period of my life, which I would should most choose to live over again, I might be tempted to point to this later period. I possess the same ardour as ever in study, and the same gaiety in company. I consider, besides, that a man of sixty five, by dying, cuts off only a few years of infirmities; and though I see many symptoms of my reputation's breaking out at last with additional lustre, I knew that I had but few years to enjoy it. It is difficult to be more detached from life than I am at present.

Despite his claimed detachment from life, Hume seemed to enjoy the last seven years of his life back in Edinburgh, with many friends with whom he found "gaiety in company." His friends were, on the whole, not dour Scots but convivial men like his old army friend Edmonstoune, with whom he could enjoy an anti-religious joke, as well as moderate Presbyterians like Blair and Robertson, for whom Hume had done some favors when he was in London. Adam Smith, too, was a good friend, though he seemed to have feared that Hume's views on religion, if he published his long-gestated *Dialogues,* might bring not only their author but also his friends into disrepute. Hume also had friendships with women, such as the sprightly Alison Cockburn, a friend of long standing, who had written to him before his return from Paris offering to find him both a suitable house and a suitable wife. Hume took up cooking in these last years and boasts in a letter about his sheep's head soup and his delicious beef with cabbage. His women friends included the young Nancy Orde, to whom he left money for a ring in his will. She was the daughter of Baron Orde, chief justice, and is reputed to be one of those

Tomb of David Hume, Edinburgh, Lothian, Scotland, by
Robert Adam (1728–1792). Courtesy of Special Collections,
Fine Arts Library, Harvard College Library.

responsible for putting up the sign "St David's Street" outside Hume's fine new house in St. Andrew's Square. It became the official name of that street, and in Dunedin, New Zealand, the Edinburgh of the south, where I write this account, a second St. David Street leads to the university.

Some of Hume's letters suggest that he may have thought of marriage until the state of his health and his increasing weakness put an end to any such plan. All his life he had been a man who loved conversation and relished friendship, while also needing time alone for writing, reading, and thinking. Hume said in *My Own Life* that this last period of his life, even when he knew he was dying, was the one he would most prefer if granted the chance to live over again, for its "ardour as ever in study, and the same gaiety in company." This, after his time as a celebrity in Paris, tells us much about what he came to value most: not literary fame and adulation but real friendship, including that of the "modest women," young and older, whom he knew and met with in Edinburgh in his last years. He enjoyed dinner parties with his friends and on one occasion was smuggled anonymously to the dinner table of Mrs. Adam, mother of Robert and James, the architects. She had forbidden them to bring home the great infidel. But once he had dined with her, she asked them who that very charming man had been. When he knew he was dying, in a letter to Adam Smith (L 2:308) he reports how he has lost five stone and tells Smith that if he does not come soon, he will find Hume to have altogether disappeared. Some well-meaning Christians tried to get him to die a Christian, for he was well known in Edinburgh, and his fatal illness soon became also well known. A candle-maker's wife called to beg him to repent. Hume received her kindly and ordered a large supply of candles from her. It was in these last months that he wrote *My Own Life,* ending it in the past tense. His sister, too, was much distressed that he was determined to die as he had lived, without the consolations of religion.

He tried to persuade his good friend Adam Smith, whose *Wealth of Nations* had appeared in the last year of Hume's life and which Hume had hailed, to undertake the publication after his death of his *Dialogues on Natural Religion,* on which he had been working for two decades. Smith refused, foreseeing how much the work might disturb religious readers. So it was left to Hume's nephew, the younger David Hume, to see it through the press in 1779, two years after Hume's peaceful death (from what may have been a liver or an intestinal tumor). Why was Hume so determined that the *Dialogues* be published, and why did his friend, Adam Smith, not help him in securing this aim?

Hume had earlier made quite clear to his reading public his rejection of the Christian religion. His "Natural History of Religion" had made all popular religions look most ridiculous, and his essay on miracles in his first *Enquiry* had targeted especially the foundation of the Christian religion. In his *History of England,* he had detailed the horrors that Christian religious fervor had wrought, both on fellow Christians and in the Crusades, on Muslims. So why did Smith think even more outrage might be caused by his *Dialogues*? I think because they attacked theism itself, the sort of belief many of Hume's own friends among the moderates in the Church of Scotland might have held, which played down revelation but kept a worship of a creator-god. This is precisely what is attacked in Hume's posthumous *Dialogues.* Smith himself may have been this sort of lukewarm Christian believer, and he foresaw how devastating Hume's examination of Christian beliefs would be to such as himself. Although Philo, the skeptic who voiced the arguments against belief in an all powerful and benevolent creator-god, at the end pretended to retreat to the comfort of "revealed" Christianity, such a stance had already been demolished by Hume in his "Natural History." So this posthumous work was the final peg in Hume's case against Christianity. It is not surprising that Smith was reluctant, nor is it surprising that Hume was determined. The surprise, if there is any, is that his nephew, David, who went on to become a fairly conservative judge and chief justice, should have seen that the *Dialogues,* however controversial, must be published. His sense of duty to his uncle, who had left this charge to him, outweighed any qualms he himself may have had about what they said. The grateful nephew proved, in this case, more faithful than the old friend. Hume's sister was pious and was very disturbed when he, a famous infidel, was reading pagan humorists like Lucian as he died. And there is no reason to think that the rest of his family, any more than his friend Adam Smith, shared his attitude to religion. He was alone, in his family and among most of his friends, not just in rejecting but in fairly strenuously opposing the religion in which they had all been reared. He died calmly and peacefully, having added in his last days some light-hearted codicils to his will.

His rejection of Christian doctrine is evident also in two essays published after his death, on suicide, defending it, and on immortality, arguing against it.

Hume had intended including them in his 1757 dissertations but had been persuaded not to, since they were so offensive to Christian believers. Burton in his biography chides Hume with the neglect, in the essay on suicide, of the effect of such an act on family and friends. But surely, as Hume had argued in the essay, no one would resort to suicide unless his life had become intolerable, and true friends would understand that (Ess 588). To keep on living an intolerable life so as not to unduly upset one's friends is not something any good friend would want one to do. In the next and final chapter, I shall consider why this anti-religious stance was one to which Hume proved, in the words of his family motto, "True to the end." His publisher, William Strahan, had written to Hume near the end, asking whether his views on a future life were not altering, as he approached death. Hume did not live to reply to Strahan, but as he had said to Boswell, when pressed on the same point a little earlier, he saw any survival after death as no more reasonable a hypothesis than that a coal, put on a blazing fire, would not burn. This reply upset Boswell, as much by the mention of fire, no doubt, as for its rejection of Christian belief. (Boswell was a great sinner and lived in dread of a future hellfire for sinners.) Hume, with calm and detachment, awaited "a speedy dissolution."

7

DEATH AND CHARACTER

To CONCLUDE HISTORICALLY *with my own character, I am, or rather was (for that is the style I must now use in speaking of myself, which emboldens me the more to speak my sentiments), I was, I say, a man of mild dispositions, of command of temper, of an open, social, and cheerful humour, capable of attachment, but little susceptible of enmity, and of great moderation in all my passions. Even my love of literary fame, my ruling passion, never soured my humour, notwithstanding my frequent disappointments. My company was not unacceptable to the young and careless, as well as to the studious and literary: and as I took a particular pleasure in the company of modest women, I had no reason to be displeased with the reception I met with from them. In a word, though most men in anywise eminent, have found reason to complain of calumny, I was never touched, or even attacked, by her baleful tooth: and though I wantonly exposed myself to the rage of both civil and religious faction, they seemed to be disarmed in my behalf of their wonted fury. My friends never had occasion to vindicate any one circumstance of my character and conduct: not but that the zealots, we may well suppose, would have been glad to invent and propagate any story to my disadvantage, but they could never find any which they thought would wear the face of probability. I cannot say there is no vanity in making this funeral oration of myself, but I hope it is not a misplaced one; and this is a matter of fact which is easily cleared and ascertained.*

April 18, 1776

Hume gave us his famous funeral oration, putting himself in the past tense and taking pride in his character rather than in his writings (though he does allow that he was in some way "eminent"). He of course exaggerates when he says his friends never had to defend him against charges of bad character: those who defended him against the charges of infidelity and immorality in Edinburgh in 1755–1756 may have felt a little offended when they read these last claims. And he had regarded Rousseau's claims about him as "calumnies" and had seemed touched by them. Quite a bit of forgetting is going on in this paragraph, and the evidence provided by earlier parts of the work show that he had felt the fury of religious faction.

Throughout his life, Hume called himself a skeptic, and in this last paragraph of *My Own Life* he boasts of his equanimity of temper. The ancient skeptics aimed to attain "ataraxia," a calm of mind, which accompanied their resignation to not knowing many of the things it is natural for us to want to know. The true skeptic sees both sides of any matter and suspends judgment, letting his actions be guided by appearances. One thing that Hume had considered very thoroughly throughout his life was the basis and the desirability of religious faith, and in particular of faith in the Christian religion. Did he suspend judgment about that? There is no doubt, I think, that Hume's study of the role of the Christian religion in British history, and his experience in youth of the effects of the Presbyterian religion on persons like himself, made him quite intransigently opposed to popular Christianity. We know little of his early breakdown in health or the role of religion-induced guilt, and rebellion against it, in causing that. But he did not underestimate the human wish to find something worthy of worship and never called himself an atheist. What he opposed was a social institution that made people feel ashamed of quite natural human desires, such as sexual desires, and that made them feel they should see themselves as essentially sinful. It was also an institution which, although preaching love, had horribly persecuted those whose version of the God of Love was in any way different from its own. It was "religious faction," hatred in the name of love, which Hume could not stomach. But he never said he knew that his religious friends and relatives were wrong in their Christian beliefs. He was a true skeptic, neither affirming nor denying the beliefs of which others were so firmly convinced.

When he was in Paris, he was a laughingstock of his philosophe friends and hosts for saying that he had never met a genuine atheist, while they, as they told him, were proud to call themselves atheists. Hume never did that and declined the label "deist" too. He thought that we could not know what the cause of the universe or our own nature was, so "agnostic," the term T. H. Huxley coined, fits him better than "atheist." But what he did claim to know was that the effects of religious zeal in human societies had been ghastly and had led to terrible religious wars and persecutions. About this he expressed no doubt whatsoever. But many of his relatives and friends prayed and found some consolation and inspiration for good works in their religious faith, and Hume never tried to change their minds about this. He asked friends like Hugh Blair not to discuss religion with him but to agree to differ. His toleration was for private devotion, not for militant and organized religion. On his deathbed he said he would like to have been around to see the churches closed down (as so many are today) and the clergy sent about their business, and he hoped his writings would play some role in bringing this about. But as far as we know, he never tried to persuade his sister, or Smith, or Blair, to renounce their religious faith. He did not share it, and he thought the churches had blood on their hands, but he understood the human urge to find some intelligent and benevolent power, supervising our often disordered human world. He managed, and managed well, without such faith, and as Smith said about him, his charity and goodness put many Christians to shame. Hume had no appreciation of music, so one reason why some of us, who share his lack of faith and his opposition to organized religion, find it difficult to altogether deplore our culture's religious past is the great music, art, and architecture which has been inspired by religious faith. If the churches being shut up were to mean that Bach chorales were to be renounced, let alone cathedrals like that at Rheims demolished, we might well hesitate.

Smith in his letter to Strahan praised the calm detached manner in which Hume met death, but this was something which did offend many Christians. To have been reading the pagan humorist Lucian on his deathbed was a fact used against Hume after his death, and many friends had to defend him posthumously. So his character of himself does overplay his independence. He did not depend on wealthy or powerful patrons (only one of his works ever bore any dedication, and that is his *Four Dissertations,* which contained his "Natural History of Religion" and was initially dedicated to the minister-playwright John Home, who was being persecuted by the Presbyterian church at the time). However, Hume had depended at first on his family for bed and board, and he often needed his good friends. Like a true skeptic, he tried to rise above the vagaries of fate, and *My Own Life* tells us how he kept bouncing back from disappointment. He says his early resolve was "to maintain unimpaired my independency, and to regard every object as contemptible, except the improvement of my talents for literature." So even when finally (after two previous attempts, in 1763 and in 1767) he retired to Edinburgh in 1769, by then "opulent," he says that he "tried what superfluity could produce, as I had formerly made an experiment of a competency." This shows a nice detachment from worldly wealth. One thing his superfluity produced was the fine house in the new St. Andrews Square. Another was his ability to help his nephews financially, as their father had earlier supported him at Ninewells.

Hume tells us that his company was acceptable to the "young and careless," and these would have included his nephews, though one doubts that Baron Hume, as one of them became, ever deserved the adjective "careless." (Baron Hume's older brother, Josey, was another matter.) Hume also saw something of the children of such friends as Gilbert Elliot, William Mure, and Lord Hertford, the last of whom who had thirteen children. Hume says that modest women liked his company, as he liked theirs. Not all his women friends, especially in Paris, were exactly modest, either in mode of life or in pretensions. Some tidying up of the record is going on in this last paragraph, and that includes what he says of his friends, some of whom, as I began this chapter by noting, had indeed had reason to come to his defense.

Besides maintaining his independence, Hume had resolved to regard everything except improvement of his literary talents as contemptible. The reception that his writings received was at first treated by him as an indicator of their worth. In his "advertisement" to the *Treatise,* he said he was determined to regard the public's judgment, whatever it be, as his best instruction. But by the time he was writing and publishing his *History,* especially after the poor reception of the first volume of it that he published, that on the early Stuarts, he seems to have written off his public as hopelessly prejudiced, and he became "callous" of their opinion. By the end he was referring to "the barbarians on the banks of the Thames." He came to rely only on his own judgment and that of a few respected literati friends in France, Scotland, and America and a few, including Gibbon, in England. A true skeptic will take neither fame nor infamy seriously, and Hume came to be as independent in his judgment about his literary talents as he prided himself on being on other matters. But when he arranged for Robert Adam to design his tomb, he wanted only his name and dates inscribed there, "leaving it to posterity to add the rest." He seemed fairly confident, in his last months, that his reputation was gaining "additional lustre," just as he seemed fairly sure that posterity's judgment would be, on the whole, favorable. He has, of course, had many critics, not only of his philosophical views and of his historical judgments, but even of his character. Birkbeck Hill found him wanting in moral courage for not being more forthright in his views about religion, and the philosopher A. E. Taylor thought him wanting in "high seriousness" and a bad influence on the young, just as Hume's contemporary James Balfour had found him to be. But his philosophy is regularly taught to the young in today's universities, and the Hume Society, renowned for its good fellowship, numbers many young people, including many women among its members. Its numbers have grown from the twenty-seven charter members in 1974, all in the United States, to 660 today, scattered all over the world. Posterity first treated his *History* as a standard work for about a century and recently has been busy adding book after book about his views, as in the philosophy journals there is a constant flow of articles about him. This little book has ranged much more widely than most Hume books, except those of his biographers, who however usually attempted less in the way of summary of his views than I have. In some ways Hume's writings were his life, or the main concern of it, but other parts of his life, such as his early study of law, his solitary exile in France as a young unpublished writer, and his later travels in Europe, all affected his writings. In this slim book I have tried to bring life and works together, guided mainly by Hume's own words. In his life he had shown the cheerfulness and undaunted spirit that he endorses as virtues in his ethics. His statue in Edinburgh shows him as a kind of Socrates, intrepid and calm. Let him have the last word (words from his "favourite performance"):

Who can dispute that a mind, which supports
a perpetual serenity and cheerfulness, a noble
dignity and undaunted spirit, a tender affection
and goodwill to all around; as it has more
enjoyment within itself, is also a more animating
and rejoicing spectacle, than if dejected with
melancholy, tormented with anxiety, irritated
with rage, or sunk into the most abject
baseness and degeneracy? (E 277)

AFTERWORD

I SAID AT THE START of this book that I wanted to share some of Hume's wisdom with a wider range of readers than those who have studied his philosophy. I have summarized some of his views, but I have not said what I find wise in them. Since not all of Hume's readers agree about what was wisdom and what was folly—in, for example, his essay on miracles, which was what raised the ire of A. E. Taylor and led him to ask whether Hume's ingeniousness was not exceeded by his perversity; or his empiricist principle, which his editor T. H. Green found, by Hume's application of it, to be reduced *ad absurdum;* or his determinist version of our wills, which even some sympathetic commentators like Terence Penelhum dislike—my findings here cannot claim to express any consensus. Hume scholars enjoy a vigorous debate, more perhaps than Hume himself did. Some even dispute that Hume's *My Own Life* should be given the authority that I have let it have. M. A. Stewart calls it mere "mischief-making" and "damage control." It is true that Hume wrote it to accompany the authorized version of his writings, which were not to include things like his "Concise Account" of his quarrel with Rousseau, nor his "Bellman's Petition," which was perhaps merely mischievous, so he left out of the account of his life some matters which were irrelevant to his authorized works. But he devotes several pages to what he did after those authorized writings were, apart from some revisions, complete—namely, his time in Paris with Lord Hertford, in London with General Conway, and his last years in Edinburgh. He knew we would want more of the life than just what influenced the writings. And he may have whitewashed his character a little, since he had at times become angrier than he seems to admit in his characterization of himself. But still, *My Own Life* is the natural place for anyone to start, to find out about Hume's life, and it is quite essential if we want to know his self-image. When it comes to labeling particular views of his as wise or foolish, however, there is bound to be disagreement. I shall say what I find wise and leave it to those who are encouraged by what I have written to read Hume for themselves to reach their own considered judgments.

The first wise move Hume made, right at the start, was to try to see what sort of animal the human animal is before working out any conclusions about how best we should live. Theists and Kantians of course will protest at my reference to humans as "animals," but the term as Hume uses it has no negative connotation, unless one regards mortality as negative. In his *Treatise* Hume looked at animal reason, animal pride, animal love, and animal sympathy in order to understand our human versions of all of these. He sees us as mammals for whom the strongest tie is that of parents for their children. We are also aggressive and acquisitive animals, who need rules and police and governments if we are to live in peace. And even when we have national governments, they go to war with one another. Hume gives us a quite unvarnished version of our nature, the problems it sets for us, and both in his account of justice and in his essays and *History,* he attends carefully to variants of our customs and our ways of letting ourselves be governed. One of his early essays was "Of the Dignity and Meanness of Human Nature," in which he speaks of the futility of collective self-disgust. The version of theism he had been reared in saw us all as miserable sinners but also saw some of us as "the elect." This attempt to combine dignity with essential sinfulness was what Hume had rejected in his youth. He accepted our mortality as an obvious fact about us, as about every other animal, and approached his own death with exemplary cheerfulness. In rejecting the doctrine of original sin, he was not denying that our behavior could be terrible—cruel, selfish, and greedy. He was quite realistic about the evil human beings have wrought, but he found that religious zealots had been as cruel and as merciless as anyone had and that their own fear of divine punishment and concern with eternal salvation tended to corrupt their character, inducing what he in his *Dialogues* called a "narrow contracted selfishness." Nor, in denying that we have immortal souls and are made in the divine image, did he deny that we had some accomplishments to be proud of, things like great literature, the printing press, Newton's science, and some tried recipes for tolerable government, even constitutional "plans of liberty." Like Herodotus, Hume thought that we make our gods in our own image, that our idea of God was of the best we find in ourselves, indefinitely enlarged—just as horses, if they had a god, would have a super-horse. Calm realism about both the good and the bad potential in human nature, including our religious proclivities, and about human mortality is the first wise thing I find in Hume's philosophy.

The second and connected wise thing is advocating resignation to living in imperfect societies and willingness to obey local customs, however fanciful their details may be, especially when it comes to established religions. As long as such customs keep us at peace with each other and do not unduly oppress some, to make life easier for others we should learn to live with them. Customs like slavery and polygamous marriage were definitely opposed by Hume, but where to draw the line between straight-out slavery and bad working conditions, or between treating wives as possessions and some degree of marital tyranny, is never easy. Only extreme tyranny justifies violent rebellion, Hume thought, but he certainly encouraged the women of his time to use what power they had to improve their social condition. His clear vision of what improvements were needed, in our life together, and his encouragement of reform by any method, short of violence, makes him, in my judgment, a wise social philosopher. Unlike Rousseau, he wrote nothing that could be used to justify the French Revolution, but what he did write justified the various reform bills in nineteenth-century Britain and, in the twentieth, the extension of suffrage to women. He was an advocate of gradual reform and of nonviolent protest against social wrongs. I think he would have admired the suffragettes, whose protest was, on their part, usually nonviolent. He had a clear vision of the power that women in principle have, by their superior knowledge of who fathered their children, and also of their inferior role in marriage, when chastity is demanded of them as if to cancel out this natural advantage. Wives, in the accepted version of marriage, renounce any hope of sexual liberty while husbands retain theirs, without losing knowledge of who their children are. In an early and later withdrawn essay on "Love and Marriage," Hume said he had considered writing a panegyric on marriage but when he looked at the facts realized it would more likely be a satire. What he wrote in the *Treatise,* in the essay on divorce, and in his second *Enquiry,* amounts indeed to a valuable satire on marriage, which should be a challenge to social philosophers to design a less unequal long-term partnership between pairs of parents, or indeed between any adults.

Hume was also a social philosopher who understood economics and how cultural goods depend on economic health. Both in his essays on trade, money, and interest and in his charting of English economic practices in his *History,* he anticipated much of what his friend Adam Smith says in *The Wealth of Nations.* It is very wise of any social philosopher to get an understanding of economics, but very few of us can hope to be the polymath that Hume was. He was also a historian philosopher, of whom there are very few.

Of course, his historical works came after his main philosophical works, and one wishes he had written more, in the light of his historical findings, than those amazingly wise appendices to the history and a last little essay on government and justice, "Of the Origin of Government," which did considerably revise what he had first said, at least about justice.

Hume's account of our reason or understanding, as grounded in our experience, particularly our sense experience, and as serving our passions, anticipated modern theories about our thought, such as functionalism and connectionism. His claim that "all the perceptions of the mind are double, and come both as impressions and as ideas," addresses the question of the sort of content our sense perceptions have, both cognitive and sensory, what today are called *qualia*. There is always more to a sense impression than what we take away from it in the form of information or conceptual content. Hume was a pioneer in cognitive science, and his views are like those of today's functionalists, who see our beliefs as serving our goals and as deriving their content from what we have learned from experience and their contribution to successful action. He did not much discuss the role of language in our thought but emphasized our ability to read each other's faces and gestures, so to sympathize with each other. He anticipated recent discoveries of our mirror neurons, when he wrote that we have a "pre-sensation" of what others are feeling from what we feel immediately in ourselves when we observe their faces. We do not need to speak to express our feelings and to communicate them to others. This expressive ability we share with other animals, and Darwin, who was a reader and admirer of Hume, was later to write a book, *The Expression of Emotion in Animals and Man,* about its importance. One place where Hume does see language playing an important role is in our assurances to one another, both in acceptance of social conventions and in giving promises to particular persons. Promise he sees to be a great invention, which extends trust from simultaneous transfer of goods or services to future transfer. Language may not be needed for thinking, in his view (since he thought other animals could learn from experience and make causal inferences), but it does vastly extend our powers of action and of cooperative action. Nietzsche later took up Hume's thoughts on just what a wonderful thing a promise can be. And those of us today who are interested in trust look back to Hume as one who saw its central importance for a society and for each person. John Rawls attributes to him what he calls "a fideism of nature," a trust that our natural faculties serve us well enough, that we do have some natural virtues and are able to invent artificial ones to extend their range in important ways. Hume saw us as instinctively trusting our vivacious sense impressions to give us knowledge of the world we live in, at least until philosophy steps in to make us into mistrustful skeptics. He saw children as instinctively trusting their parents, teachers, and friends during their "long and helpless infancy," which he so rightly stresses. Hume saw the importance, for us, of having conventions or social agreements, so we can trust each other in particular matters, and of our having invented ways, such as contract, by which we can also trust strangers and trust sources of information, such as maps and history books. He took his own beliefs about Julius Caesar as a case in point, in which he trusts a long chain of testifiers, and has faith in the "fidelity of Printers and Copyists." (T 146). What a good time he would have, if with us today, discussing the trustworthiness of Wikipedia and Google.

One must include Hume's brilliant account of a social convention, which I discussed and quoted in Chapter 2, on the list of his wise teachings. It is a most impressive display of mutual trust when such a general agreement is reached and entered into, displaying both our expressive powers, since our sense of common interest and our willingness must be expressed to be known, and our cooperative ability, our power to work together, and to do so to enable other more specific forms of trust with specific others. Later writers on convention and cooperation, such as David Lewis and Russell Hardin, have hailed Hume here as founding father.

The last wise feature of Hume's thought that I will mention is his "true scepticism," his avoidance of advancing theses on controversial matters which are claimed as gospel truth, where we are asked just to trust his say-so. He had definite views and preferences, but he tolerated those with different views, as long as they did not try to ram them down his throat. His posthumous essay "The Immortality of the Soul" makes it quite clear that he sees no good reason for such a belief, but of course he cannot be sure it is false, so he simply lists what he sees to be the reasons for rejecting it, without calling defenders of the doctrine either fools or hypocrites, though he did think professions of religious belief were apt to go along with some hypocrisy. He may himself have advanced views which had less than compelling evidence, as in his own theory about our minds, and there may be some tension between his official skepticism and his naturalist "science of man." He was willing to reconsider matters on which he had written and sometimes to alter or retract. He said at the start of the *Treatise* that he would use the public's judgment as his best instruction. He was an infidel, but he did not preach atheism. His second most famous "funeral oration," Adam Smith's letter about him to Hume's publisher William Strahan, which was published along with *My Own Life*, ended: "I have always considered him, both in his lifetime and in his death, as approaching as nearly to the idea of a perfectly wise and virtuous man, as perhaps the nature of human frailty will permit." This came from a friend who did believe in the Great Judge and who was unwilling to be associated in any way with Hume's openly unbelieving *Dialogues on Natural Religion*. Hume was a famous infidel with famous friends who were believers. But he valued his friendships more than he cared about his friends' agreement with his views. One very wise thing he wrote—and this time I really will let him have the last word—was "Destroy love and friendship, and what remains in the world worth accepting?"

ANNOTATED BIBLIOGRAPHY

FURTHER READING

ACKNOWLEDGMENTS

NAME INDEX

SUBJECT INDEX

ANNOTATED BIBLIOGRAPHY

(Listing all of the books referred to in the Introduction, but not those in the remainder of the text.)

Berkeley, George. *A Treatise Concerning the Principles of Human Knowledge.* Dublin: Aaron Rhames for Jeremy Pepyat, 1710. This and other works by Berkeley are available in an Everyman edition, edited by Michael Ayers (London: Dent, 1985). Berkeley's views, especially on abstraction and on our evidencè for the existence of material things, influenced Hume.

Burton, John Hill. *Life and Correspondence of David Hume,* 2 vols. Edinburgh: W. Tait, 1846. This was the second life of Hume to be written, the first being Ritchie's.

Capaldi, Nicholas. *The Philosophy of David Hume.* Boston: Twayne Publishers, 1975. An account of Hume's philosophical thought, with an informative chronology of events just before and during his life.

Graham, Roderick. *The Great Infidel: A Life of David Hume.* East Linton, Scotland: Tuckwell Press, 2004; paperback ed., Edinburgh: Birlinn Press, 2006. A lively and well-illustrated account of Hume's life.

Greig, J. Y. T. *David Hume*. London: Jonathan Cape, 1931. Reprint, Oxford: Oxford University Press, 1983. Perhaps the best and most sympathetic account of Hume's life, but without a detailed account of his thought. Greig, a literary scholar, also edited Hume's letters.

Hill, George Birkbeck. *Letters of David Hume to William Strahan*. Oxford: Clarendon Press, 1888. Hill collected Hume's letters to his publisher, written toward the end of his life.

Huxley, Thomas Henry. *Hume, with Helps to the Study of Berkeley*. New York: D. Appleton, 1897. Huxley, Darwin's "bulldog," likes Hume's account of our nature and its continuity with animal nature.

Knight, William. *Hume*. London: Kennikat Press, 1886. A general introduction to Hume's philosophy.

Merrill, Kenneth. *The A–Z of Hume's Philosophy*. Lanham, MD: Rowman and Littlefield, 2010. This little book has entries on some main topics in Hume's philosophy.

Mossner, Ernest C. *The Life of David Hume,* 2nd ed. Oxford: Clarendon Press, 1980. The most complete English language account we have of Hume's life. Mossner was, like Greig, primarily a literary scholar, and though he does give some account of Hume's thought, since it is because of it that we want a biography, as he says in his preface, "the man predominates."

Orr, James. *David Hume, and His Influence on Philosophy and Theology*. New York: Scribner's, 1903. Orr was a theologian, so is not in agreement with Hume's views, but is quite sympathetic to Hume the man.

Price, J. V. *David Hume*. Boston: Twayne Publishers, 1968; updated ed. 1991. Price treats Hume as a man of letters, so discusses all his writings and attends to his style. Price also wrote a book entitled *The Ironic Hume* (Austin: University of Texas Press, 1965).

Price, Richard. *A Review of the Principal Questions and Difficulties of Morals*. 1758, later editions 1769 and 1787. In the third edition the title is shortened to *A Review of the Principal Questions of Morals,* which is that used in the modern edition, edited by D. D. Raphael (Oxford: Clarendon Press, 1948). Hutcheson, rather than Hume, is the main target of Price's criticism. Price was a Unitarian preacher and believed that God-given reason shows us what is right and wrong.

Ritchie, Thomas Edward. *An Account of the Life and Writings of David Hume, Esq.* London: T. Cadell and W. Davies, 1909; reprint, Bristol: Thoemmes, 1990. This incorporates some correspondence and republishes some of Hume's essays.

Smellie, William. *Literary and Characteristical Lives of John Gregory, M.D., Henry Home, Lord Kames, David Hume, Esq., and Adam Smith, L.L.D.* Edinburgh: A. Smellie, 1800. Smellie was a printer and a friend of Lord Kames, whose life is also discussed in these memoirs.

Stephen, Sir Leslie. *English Thought in the Eighteenth Century,* 2 vols. London: Smith Elder and Company, 1881.

In volume 1, chapter 6, Stephen devotes forty pages to Hume, emphasizing his challenge to religious belief.

Streminger, Gerhardt. *David Hume, Sein Leben und Sein Werk*. Paderborn: Ferdinand Schöningh, 1994. Perhaps the most complete account yet of Hume's life, his times, and his work, with rich illustrations. Not yet in English translation.

FURTHER READING

Árdal, Páll. *Passion and Value in Hume's* Treatise. Edinburgh: Edinburgh University Press, 1966. The first book to look at the importance of *Treatise,* Book 2, "Of the Passions," for understanding its sequel, Book 3, "Of Morals."

Ayer, Alfred Jules. *Hume: A Very Short Introduction.* Oxford: Oxford University Press, 2000. A little gem about Hume by an original philosopher who was much influenced by him.

Baier, Annette C. *A Progress of Sentiments: Reflections on Hume's* Treatise. Cambridge, MA: Harvard University Press, 1991. This book tries to show the unity of Hume's *Treatise.*

Fogelin, Robert J. *Hume's Skepticism in the* Treatise of Human Nature. London: Routledge & Kegan Paul, 1985; and *Hume's Skeptical Crisis: A Textual Study.* Oxford: Oxford University Press, 2009. Fine studies of the skeptical strain in Hume's thought.

Garrett, Don. *Cognition and Commitment in Hume's Philosophy.* New York: Oxford University Press, 1997. An influential account of Hume's philosophical thought.

Laird, John. *Hume's Philosophy of Human Nature*. London: Methuen, 1932. A careful and balanced account of Hume's philosophy.

Loeb, Louis E. *Stability and Justification in Hume's* Treatise. Oxford: Oxford University Press, 2002. Loeb gives a sympathetic account of Hume's views on justified belief, in book 1 of the *Treatise*.

Mackie, J. L. *Hume's Moral Theory*. London: Routledge & Kegan Paul, 1980. A sympathetic study of Hume's moral theory, with some attention to his predecessors.

MacNabb, D. I. C. *David Hume, His Theory of Knowledge and Morality*. London: Hutchinson's University Library, 1951. An excellent introduction.

Passmore, J. A. *Hume's Intentions*. Cambridge: Cambridge University Press, 1952. An influential examination of several strands in Hume's thought.

Penelhum, Terence. *Themes in Hume: Self, Will, Religion*. Oxford: Oxford Univerity Press, 2003. A sympathetic presentation of some of Hume's views, from one who does not always agree with Hume.

Rawls, John. *Lectures on the History of Moral Philosophy,* edited by Barbara Herman. Cambridge, MA: Harvard University Press, 2000. Rawls gives an appreciative account of Hume's moral philosophy, especially his account of justice.

Russell, Paul. *The Riddle of Hume's* Treatise: *Skepticism, Naturalism, and Irreligion*. Oxford: Oxford University

Press, 2008. This book shows how irreligion permeates Hume's *Treatise*, despite the fact that in it he barely mentions religion.

Smith, Norman Kemp. *The Philosophy of David Hume*. London: Macmillan, 1941. This work emphasizes Hume's debt to Hutcheson, and Hume's theory of natural belief.

Stroud, Barry. *Hume*. London: Routledge and Kegan Paul, 1977. A deeply philosophical meditation on Hume's main ideas, probing his skepticism.

ACKNOWLEDGMENTS

Since I wanted this book to be accessible to readers who are not professional philosophers, I asked two of my sisters, Beverley White, a former high school teacher of English and history, and Jennifer Galbraith, who was a nurse, to read it and tell me which bits they had trouble understanding. They kindly obliged, and so I then rewrote a few passages. My nephew Alastair Galbraith, who is a musician, painter, and has a degree in philosophy, also read it but liked it as it was and was most encouraging. Then I had helpful advice from former student Christopher Williams and anonymous readers for Harvard University Press. To all these people, as well as to Hannah Wong of Harvard University Press, who helped especially with the illustrations, and John Donohue and Julie Palmer-Hoffman of Westchester Book Services, who did the copyediting, I express my sincere gratitude.

NAME INDEX

Adam, Robert, 119, 131

Addison, Joseph, 58

Alembert, Jean le
Rond d', 108

Allestree, Joseph, 9

Annandale, Marquis of,
35, 60

Ayer, A. J., 1

Balfour, James, 73, 74, 75, 131

Bayle, Pierre, 20

Beattie, James, 75

Becket, Thomas, Arch-
bishop, 4, 98

Bennett, Jonathan, 5

Berkeley, George, 1, 23, 24,
31

Blair, Hugh, 88, 92, 97, 113,
117, 127, 128

Blanc, Jean-Bernard, Abbé
Le. *See* Le Blanc, Jean-
Bernard, Abbé

Boswell, James, 9, 114, 123

Bouffleurs, Hippolyte de
Saujon, Comtesse de, 97,
105–107, 108–109, 110–111,
112

Burton, John Hill, 1, 100–
101, 123

Butler, Bishop Joseph, 18,
65

Calvin, John, 75

Capaldi, Nicholas, 1

Catherine II, Empress of
Russia, 109

Cauldfeild, James, Lord
Charlemont, 67

Cauldfeild family, 112

Cicero, Marcus, 7, 10

Clarke, Samuel, 12

Cockburn, Alison, 117

Conway, General, 103, 112, 113, 135

Coutts, John, Provost, 62, 63

Cromwell, Oliver, 89, 90, 91

Dalrymple, Sir David, 89, 93

Darwin, Charles, 29, 141

Defoe, Daniel, 78

Descartes, René, 16, 17, 19, 20, 21, 22, 24, 26, 28, 31, 36, 37

Diderot, Denis, 108–109

Douglas, Archibald, 113–115

Douglas, Lady Jane, 114

Dudgeon, William, 12

Edmonstoune, James, 117

Edward I, King of England, 99

Edward II, King of England, 99

Edwy, King of England, 99

Elgiva, Queen of England, 99

Elizabeth I, Queen of England, 86, 93, 94–95

Elliot, Anne, 95–96

Elliot, Peggy, 95–96

Elliot, Sir Gilbert, 12, 88, 130

Falconer, Sir David, 6, 7

Fodor, Jerry, 53

Franklin, Benjamin, 4, 98

Galbraith, Agnes, 12, 36

Gibbon, Edward, 131

Graham, Roderick, 1

Green, T. H., 131, 134

Greig, J. Y. T., 1, 2, 14

Hamilton, James George, Duke of, 114

Harris, James, 2

Herodotus, 137

Hobbes, Thomas, 20, 71

Holbach, Paul-Henry
    Thiry, Baron d', 107
Home, Henry, Lord Kames,
    18, 62, 91, 92, 96
Home, John (the philoso-
    pher's brother), 6, 7, 9, 10,
    14, 16, 55, 57, 66–67, 71, 86
Home, Joseph (the philoso-
    pher's father), 6–8, 45
Home, Joseph (the philoso-
    pher's nephew), 129, 130
Home, Katherine (the phi-
    losopher's mother), 6, 7,
    8, 10, 13–14, 16, 55, 57, 72
Hume, David, Baron (the
    philosopher's nephew),
    122, 129, 130
Hurd, Dr., 85
Huxley, T. H., 1, 29, 54, 127

Irvine, Peggy (Hume's
    housekeeper), 88

James I, King of England,
    90, 93, 94–95
Junius, 113

Knight, William, 1

Le Blanc, Jean-Bernard,
    Abbé, 72, 89, 96
Locke, John, 12, 23, 24, 31

Mansfield, Lord, 114
Merrill, Kenneth, 1
Middleton, Rev. Conyers,
    56
Millar, Andrew, 57, 85, 96
Montesquieu, Baron de, 67,
    89, 97
Mossner, E., 1, 2
Mure, William, Baron of
    Caldwell, 83, 95, 114, 130

Nietzsche, Friedrich, 141

Orr, William, 1, 13, 14

Price, J. V., 1
Price, Richard, 1

Ramsay, Allan, 88, 91
Ramsay, Michael, 16–17
Ritchie, Thomas Edward, 1
Robertson, William, 117
Rousseau, Jean-Jacques, 89, 97, 109, 110–111, 135, 138

Smellie, William, 1
Stephen, Lesley, 1
Strahan, William, 1, 96, 123, 128, 144
Streminger, Gerhard, 1, 2

Warburton, William, Bishop, 85, 96, 115

SUBJECT INDEX

Note: Page numbers in *italics* indicate figures.

Abilities, 47, 48, 74

"Abstract" of *A Treatise of Human Nature,* 62–63

Animals, 19, 20, 28, 29, 49, 69, 136, 141

Approbation, 40, 48

Artifice, 43, 44, 45, 46

Assault, 46

Association of ideas, 23, 26, 27, 32, 51, 52, 62

Assurance, 43, 44, 141

Atheism, 108, 126–127

Austria, 61, 65–66

Belief: nature and basis of, 24, 34–35, 37, 50, 52, 68, 69, 78, 79; religious belief, 26, 60, 108, 126–127, 143

Benevolence, 46

Berwick, 8

Bristol, Hume's time there, 11, 15, 80

Carinthia, 67

Cause, our idea of, 21, 22, 26, 27, 62, 63–64, 68, 69

Cheerfulness, 46, 132, 133, 136

Children, 44–45, 46, 73, 136

Chirnside, 8

Christianity, 12, 82, 98, 121–123, 126

Consciousness, 24

Contiguity, 23, 24, 26, 68

Contract, 42–43, 46, 142

Convention, 40, 41–44, 72, 141–143

Courage, 46, 48

Cruelty, 46, 47, 80

Customs, 16, 45, 76–79, 88, 100, 136, 137–138

Danube River, 65

Death: of Hume, 120; Hume's attitude to, 20, 37, 123, 136; of Hume's mother, 72

Desire, 36–37, 39, 126

Dialogues on Natural Religion, 12, 64–65, 117, 120–122, 137, 144

Dishonesty, 47

Dissertations, Hume's, 61, 62, 70, 81, 82, 123, 129

Divorce, 44, 58, 139

Doubt, 31–32, 127

Douglas cause, 113–115

Duty, 39

Economics, 61, 76, 139

Edinburgh, 4, 6, 10, 31, 35, 50, 55, 57, 60, 62, 73, 86, 87–88, 91–92, 93, 103, 111, 114–115, 116, 117, 119–120, 125, 129, 132, 135

Education, Hume's, 7, 10, 20

Eloquence, 31, 46, 58, 60; of Rousseau, 97

Enquiry Concerning Human Understanding, 56, 60, 61, 63–64, 67–68, 69–70, 74, 121

Enquiry Concerning the Principles of Morals, An, 57–58, 61, 71–75, 107, 110, 139

Essays, Hume's, 2, 19, 20, 55, 56, 57, 60, 66, 76–80, 81, 83, 122, 136, 139

Experience, 21, 49–50, 51, 62, 140

Expression, 31, 41, 53, 86, 98, 141

Fictions, 30
Fraud, 44
Freedom: of the press, 58; of speech, 77
Friendship, 45, 103, 105, 117, 119, 123, 144

Gain, 72. *See also* Interest
Generosity, 41, 46, 49
Gratitude, 46

History of England, 3, 6, 9, 20, 81, 83, 84, 85, 86, 88, 89, 90–91, 93–95, 99–101, 107, 121, 126, 130, 132, 136, 139, 140
Hume Society, 5

Ideas, 20, 21, 23, 24, 25, 29, 39, 51, 67, 68, 140
Identity, personal, 40, 67, 69
Immorality, charges of against Hume, 91–92, 125
Impressing of seamen, 77–81

Impressions, 25–26, 30, 31, 51, 68, 69, 140, 142
Incest, 8
Inference, 21, 22, 29, 38, 63, 68
Instinct, 27, 69
Integrity, 72
Interest, 40, 41, 44, 45, 48, 76, 84, 139, 143
Italy, 56, 67

Jack's Land, 88
James Court, *87*
Justice, 10, 16, 40–42, 46, 48, 72, 136, 140; divine, 64; to Hume, 5

Kantians, 135
Knowledge: of paternity, 138–139; of self and world, 30–32, 68–70, 142

La Flèche, 16–18
Language, 19–20, 29, 140–141

Laws: enacted, 77, 79; of
    nature, 17–18, 68, 71
Liberty: civil, 58, 77, 86, 137;
    of the human will, 37, 70;
    of religion, 81; sexual, 139
London, 16, 18, 56, 57, 85,
    93, 95, 97, 105, 112, 113,
    114–115, 117, 135

Memory, 25, 51, 68
Mirroring of minds, 33
Morals, Hume's version of,
    40–49, 57–58, 71–76, 135–
    139, 141–143

Necessity: of our actions
    and passions, 37–38,
    70–71; our experience of,
    22–23
Ninewells (the family es-
    tate), 8, 11, 16, 35, 54, 56,
    71, 86

Paris, 16, 102–103, 104–112,
    127, 135

Passions, 18–19, 20–21,
    25, 31, 32–37, 39, 48,
    49, 61, 62, 70–71, 73,
    81, 140; Hume's own,
    124
Perceptions, 24–26, 30–
    31, 32, 50–52, 62, 69,
    140
Promise, 42–43, 141

Rheims, 15, 16, 128
Rhine River, 65
Riddle's Close, 86

Sexual love, 8, 35–36
Skepticism, 21, 27, 29–32,
    62, 143
Sympathy, 14, 19, 33, 36, 40,
    47, 49, 136

Thames River, 131
Trust, 21, 31, 42–43, 141–
    143
Truth, 29, 31, 34

Understanding, human, 20, 28, 30, 56, 74, 140; and morality, 49. See also *Enquiry Concerning Human Understanding*

Vienna, 61, 66

War, 61, 85, 99, 136; of American independence, 79; of Austrian Succession, 61; English civil, 90

Whitadder Rver, 8

Yvandeau, 16, *17*